HOW TO BE
A CITIZEN

C. L. SKACH

HOW TO BE A CITIZEN

LEARNING TO BE CIVIL WITHOUT THE STATE

BASIC BOOKS

New York

Basic Books

Hachette Book Group

1290 Avenue of the Americas, New York, NY 10104

www.basicbooks.com

Printed Canada

First Edition: July 2024

Published by Basic Books, an imprint of Hachette Book Group, Inc. The Basic Books name and logo is a registered trademark of the Hachette Book Group.

The Hachette Speakers Bureau provides a wide range of authors for speaking events. To find out more, go to hachettespeakersbureau.com or email HachetteSpeakers@hbgusa.com.

Basic books may be purchased in bulk for business, educational, or promotional use. For more information, please contact your local bookseller or the Hachette Book Group Special Markets Department at special .markets@hbgusa.com.

The publisher is not responsible for websites (or their content) that are not owned by the publisher.

Print book interior design by Amy Quinn.

Library of Congress Cataloging-in-Publication Data

Names: Skach, C. L., 1967– author.

Title: How to be a citizen : learning to be civil without the state / C. L. Skach.

Description: First edition. | New York : Basic Books, [2024] | Includes bibliographical references and index.

Identifiers: LCCN 2023058426 | ISBN 9781541605534 (hardcover) | ISBN 9781541605541 (ebook)

Subjects: LCSH: Civics. | Citizenship. | Quality of life.

Classification: LCC JF801 .S544 2024 | DDC 323.6/5—dc23/eng/20240301

LC record available at https://lccn.loc.gov/2023058426

ISBNs: 9781541605534 (hardcover), 9781541605541 (ebook)

MRQ

Printing 1, 2024

For Demara and Raphael

Contents

Darkness fled, light shone, and order from disorder sprung.

—John Milton, *Paradise Lost*, 1667

Preface

I CAN REMEMBER THE EXACT DAY I FINALLY LOST MY faith in formal rules—in the law. It was around the time I learned to do U-turns in an armoured SUV at fifty miles per hour and lived to eat my day's ration. It was around the time that I practised dodging explosive devices planted on the roads of Amman, becoming proficient enough to make it back in time for a shower and a glass of Lebanese wine before bed.

This was, of course, the easy part. It was the autumn of 2008, and I had just graduated from a two-week survival course in the desert, where Jordanian soldiers and UN security forces simulated terrorist activities to prepare me for, among other things, constitution writing. I had flown out to Amman from London, just before my teaching duties were to begin for the academic year. I was the newly appointed professor of comparative government and law at Oxford, and I would be taking the five-hour flight a few times over the next year, between tutorials and lectures, returning proudly to share my experience with my students.

The morning that I passed my training, a UN officer with an accent from the American South congratulated me as he plucked out a few strands of my hair by the root. This was not a hazing ritual. It was a way of collecting my DNA in case my body was later found in otherwise unidentifiable parts.

I was now ready for the real part of my job as a 'constitutional expert', as they called me. Heading this time into Baghdad, I had been invited by the UN Assistance Mission for Iraq to work with Iraqis and Kurds in the government's Committee for Constitutional Reform.

Our plane that day was far from full. Some of my group had failed the course and were sent home. Others had left early, needing psychological counselling from the trauma of the survival course alone. I sat on that old twin-prop that day, destination Baghdad International, with former counsel for the US government, academic advisors from the United Kingdom who nudged Scotland and Wales towards devolution, and many junior and some senior UN officers from countries all over the world, some of them leaving families behind to take high-paying jobs in a war zone.

I was eager to go. Not for the money. As a short-term consultant with a different day job, I wasn't being paid much. But as a constitutional scholar, a professor, I thought I had reached the top of my game. As one of my students at Oxford put it, 'You are writing constitutions, Professor Skach; it doesn't get any better than this.' Constitutions are, after all, *the* most important laws in a democracy, in a country governed by and for the people. They set the rules of the political game, telling us whether a country is unitary or federal, whether it is secular or has an established church. They tell us how our political leaders will be chosen, how and when we can change them, who will represent us and make decisions for our governance. And they tell us not only what our rights are as individuals and as members of identity groups, but also how our individual countries order these rights in a hierarchy based on our nation's values; and how our government is going to prevent these rights from being trampled on. That's why constitutions are often known as 'higher law'.

This wasn't my first time advising a foreign country on constitutional issues. I had been a dedicated disciple of the law and had published work about constitutions early in my career, first as a young graduate student and with my academic supervisor at Columbia University, and later as a professor at Harvard University, I had gone to Madrid to address former presidents and prime ministers, travelled frequently to established or emerging European democracies to meet with members of constitutional review countries or constitutional courts, and welcomed MPs from other continents who visited my office to discuss what I considered perilous constitutions and ways to build more stable legal architecture. I had spent my academic life talking about which constitutions could help democracy flourish, and I was now moving to Oxford to say it again, accepting invitations to advise, teach, and preach the value of good laws.

Iraq was without a doubt my most dangerous and challenging mission to date. The Iraqis and Kurds, under the auspices of the United Nations, had invited me because they wanted to know how to set their oil-rich country up in a way that encouraged them all to share the vast supplies of oil and gas that were found in only small pockets of the country. I had seen how such revenue sharing had worked in countries like the United States and Canada and Brazil.

These were all federated countries, where power is constitutionally divided between regions (or states), with a central government controlling some areas of policy but not all of them. Iraq was a complex country with a complicated ethnic, religious, and linguistic mix of peoples, with most of the country's natural resources located in Kurdish territory. If those peoples wanted to remain together as a state, unitary or federal, they would all have to share. But this was easier said and theorised than done.

The Iraqis were considering the merits of moving to a specific type of federal system to hold their country together. I, and quite a few others, thought that if the other Iraqis could accept Kurdish autonomy in certain areas of policy, including language, and if in exchange the Kurds could accept sharing a reasonable percentage of their wealth from the oil and gas with the rest of Iraq, there would be less tension overall and fewer Kurdish calls for independence. No other region in Iraq would enjoy such autonomy vis-à-vis Baghdad. But some evidence from other countries told us that no other region would apparently need to.[1]

This arrangement, which we call asymmetrical federalism, seemed to work in countries like Spain, where violent separatist movements lost clout among the population when the central Spanish government gave the Basques and Catalans more control over their regions. Basque and Catalan children could be educated in their regional languages rather than in Castilian Spanish. Elderly Basques and Catalans could read street signs in the languages they learned as children, rather than Spanish. The Basques and Catalans could then feel that their subcultures and histories were respected. This, we believed, kept them from wanting to blow politicians up in Madrid. We believed it kept Spain together.[2]

As I typed out the notes for my first meeting, arranging my data neatly on a PowerPoint slide, our plane hit some turbulence. I put away my laptop and closed my eyes. I tried to imagine what might await me in Iraq. Former colleagues who had been there had shared their stories, embellished with enough detail to elicit envy. Working in a war zone, writing laws and constitutions in particular, was something very few of us had done. The mere thought of participating in some constitutional founding was exciting. Maybe, if they liked what I said, I would be helping to write this higher law.

But I really had no idea.

I had no idea that within only a few weeks, I would return to the lobby of the Méridien Hotel in Amman that I had left only days before, this time scratched, covered in dirt, and smelling of sewage, from my work in Baghdad helping to design a constitution. And that this would be only the beginning.

I remember, very clearly, that horrific morning. Asleep in my camp in the International Zone, I was awakened at dawn by a terrible sound, followed by a violent shake. Our camp had been hit by a 240-millimeter rocket, meant for our neighbours at the US Embassy but falling short and hitting us hard. My survival instinct and two weeks of training kicked in, and I reached not for my clothes but for my helmet and metal jacket, snatching up my grab bag: a small sack with basic supplies and cash. I sat there in the darkness, in underwear and protective equipment, in my sandbagged room, waiting. How many were hurt? How many were dead? Would we be captured? Killed?

I thought, *So this is constitution writing.*

A knock at my door made me jump. My colleague, a father of two young children living back in North America, stood there. He was OK and had come to see whether

I was. He told me what had happened, and that we had no more electricity in the camp and no more running water. We were now going to be evacuated by tanks to a local Iraqi school which had recently been converted into a UN base. As we awaited ambulances, the camp's administrators briefed us on the attack: three people were dead, thirteen injured. We got off lightly, they said; it could have been much worse, and they remembered when it was.[3]

I've thought about that moment ever since and will do so for the rest of my life. I thought about it later that very day, while sloshing through sewage in the converted Iraqi school, where we, the survivors, shared a very limited supply of bottled water, and the UN's Bangladeshi cooks—those who survived the attack—tried to put something together for us to eat. I thought about it later again that day, as I climbed into a tank with three heavily armed American soldiers, as they drove me down sniper alley to Baghdad International Airport. I thought about it as I gratefully sipped the orange Gatorade they handed me and looked out the tiny window at this cradle of civilisation.

I left that alley feeling not only traumatised but guilty. For at that moment, the faces of the sheiks I had met, of the Iraqi and Kurdish ministers who had welcomed me and given me black lime tea, came back to me, and I realised that nothing or no one could help these people but themselves. No law, no rule. And any constitution that I or others might try to encourage them to adopt might possibly make things worse, and perhaps already had. Because laws and rules and constitutions are in the end much like human-to-human stem cell transplants. Without the pre-transplant conditioning therapy which prepares the patient, especially patients with long-standing medical problems, the complications of introducing foreign bodies can be catastrophic. So, I now thought, it could be with laws.[4]

It was there, in the tank surrounded by three American soldiers, that my career changed. There I finally acknowledged what I had always felt but suppressed: that higher laws, and rules more generally, can themselves be the seeds of order's own destruction.

Part I

THE PROBLEM

Introduction

M Y OWN LIFE AS A LAW-PROMOTING ADULT PROBA-
bly began with the fall of the Berlin Wall. I had
just finished my undergraduate degree, and all around
me the world was opening up. Pinochet had just lost the
plebiscite on the continuation of his dictatorship, and the
Southern Cone of South America was moving away from
its military men. Mikhail Gorbachev, in a different hemi-
sphere, had recently announced *glasnost*—his policy of
open discussion of the political, economic, and social state
of the Soviet Union. And I, as a young woman starting a
PhD, could not help but be fascinated by the possibilities
that all this democratic experimentation promised. Living
in New York only fed that curiosity. We students spent

long days on Columbia University's tree-lined, gated, and guarded strip of land between Broadway and Amsterdam Avenue—a flattened ivory tower, smack in the middle of a complex, diverse metropolis. My fascination began on day one. The corridors of the International Affairs Building at 124th Street were plastered with urgent-looking signs announcing, practically shouting, the cancellation of certain courses and the mad race to carve new ones. In that 'TBA' nature of our world order in the early 1990s, Soviet Law was cancelled, to be replaced by Law-Making in the Former Soviet Space. 'Communist' in many of the titles was changed to 'Post-communist', or something similar. Command Economy was now Economies in Transition. And so forth. Here we were, in a living laboratory, where before our very eyes old rules and authority structures crumbled, as countries in this vast region of the world began yet another metamorphosis, scrambling, first and foremost, to craft new rules and new laws. The edifice of the Cold War, which we had grown up believing would be settled catastrophically by nuclear weapons, was now being dismantled like a Potemkin village, one law at a time. The temptation for those interested in promoting democracy and crafting better laws, democratic laws, and constitutions full of rights and liberties was simply irresistible.

In the first year of my PhD, I wrote a paper with my supervisor that would become a part of this process. The work would solidify me as a card-carrying rule promoter, a believer in the idea that having the right rules, providing the right incentives for humans through the correctly chosen rules, was the way to carve good democracies and great citizens. Working late into the night, fuelled by good Ethiopian food and my brother's late-night deliveries of Ben & Jerry's, we managed to dig up some of the first evidence of a remarkable correlation: if you wanted to ensure that your young democracy became a stable—or what we academics call consolidated—democracy, you wanted a parliamentary constitution and not a presidential one. We had data from around the world to show that, when people became frustrated with their directly elected presidents either because they governed poorly, or because they didn't produce the policies citizens needed, or because they were fighting with the majority in the parliament and there was deadlock, there were only two ways to remove these leaders outside of an election—and both were costly. The first was through the lengthy legal process known as impeachment which, as we know from the United States, is both rare and divisive. Or there's the quicker but bloodier solution—a coup. The latter had become endemic in the presidential systems of Africa and Latin America where military men became political players—places that had taken the US presidential constitution as inspiration.[1]

Of course, parliamentary constitutions did also fail, just not as often, it seemed. But the more I began to look under the skin of these places, these polities that were plot points in our graphs, the more I began to wonder whether just changing the rules was really the answer. It might have been the summer I spent in Rio de Janeiro and Brasilia, meeting with former military leaders and trying to understand whether parliamentary rules would work in a country that, historically, was drawn to strong, charismatic leadership—the kind of caudillo who could deliver independence from a colonising power. In that breathtakingly beautiful country, with its equally beautiful people, the Gini coefficient, a standard measure of income inequality, regularly hovers around a very unequal 50 per cent, where zero is perfect equality.[2] Deeply polarised in terms of income but also troubled by great divisions between rural and urban areas, Brazil's complex social, economic, and geographic landscape led to the kind of schism that can facilitate widespread corruption and extreme fluctuations between apathy and activism, fuelling the rise of charismatic but problematic leaders.[3]

Or it might have been the year and a half that I spent in Heidelberg, researching the causes of the fall of Weimar Germany, which had been one of the most progressive in existence in its time. I studied that constitution under the *Ginkgo biloba* trees that Goethe was so fond of. At the time I believed that an important element of the Weimar Republic's demise was the coincidence of fatal rules in its constitution, including the famous Article 48, an emergency-decree power that enabled presidents, with the help of the armed forces, if needed, to take the vaguely defined 'measures necessary' during times of crisis.[4] But my

German friends and colleagues seemed more persuaded by historical voices at home who wondered whether Weimar's problems had more to do with that republic being a complicated social fabric on the eve of economic crisis and at a critical juncture in world history—and so a democracy without democrats.[5]

It might have even been the bitter cold February I spent in Moscow, interviewing human rights activists and government ministers, including Galina Starovoytova, Yeltsin's minister for ethnic affairs, who spoke generously with me in a Pizza Hut across from the Duma and whose assassination I would read about only a few months later. As she explained to me how difficult it was to work with many of Russia's new leaders, who were not 'team players', the awareness grew in me that rules and their incentive structures were one thing, personalities and attitudes another.[6]

With each real-world experience, my doubts about the power of laws mounted.

As a professor of government and law, and a practitioner advising foreign governments and educating their elites, I have perhaps been in denial about what I have known for a long time—that democracy isn't working well. Anywhere. In spite of a lot of work on getting the laws right. It is something we in the universities and think tanks have been documenting and describing for decades. At first, in the 1980s, we were hopeful as we watched South American dictatorships open up after years of brutal repression.

But within a decade, these transitions to democracy in the Southern Cone stalled, resulting in what the Argentine scholar Guillermo O'Donnell coined 'delegative democracy': partial democracies led by presidents who were freely elected but who behaved more like caudillos than accountable leaders.[7]

Then we all triumphed at the fall of the Berlin Wall in '89, only to watch right-wing populists, like Fidesz in Hungary and the Law and Justice party in Poland, slowly infest central and eastern Europe in the 2000s, infecting the region with xenophobic messages of intolerance, including outrageous statements and policies aimed at Jews, Roma, and the LGBTQ+ community.[8] We sat mesmerised as peoples across the Arab world fought for their democratic spring in the early 2010s—then saw their efforts result in a cold, bloody Arab Winter, with civil wars in Syria, Libya, and Yemen. Here, the popular movements were crushed not only by those in power but also by counterrevolutionary groups within society who resisted the ambiguity of change.[9] We also watched citizens reject the European Constitution—reject the chance for a 'We the Peoples of the United Europe' to come together and make a unique, codified commitment to one another; and then years later, we lived through Brexit and the uncertainty of Europe's social and economic future as parts of the Continent started moving back into their pre-union corners. With Russia's invasion of Ukraine on Europe's doorstep, we were both horrified and dumbstruck, but then we just got on with our lives as the war and its refugees became routine. We were sitting idle as Old Europe saw a re-emergence of hatred towards 'the other', some even filmed without acting, like tourists at a horror theme park. In the midday sunshine of an Italian coastal town, a street vendor— Alika Ogorchukwu—was even beaten to death with his own walking stick as people passed by.[10] This is what our societies had become.

But it wasn't only society that didn't behave well. Back in the United States, we were horrified at the ways 'democratic' law and order failed Rodney King, a citizen whose basic human rights should have been protected by his country's constitution and its state machinery. Instead, those rights were violated by those members of the state we entrusted to protect him, as would happen again, with Eric Garner, Michael Brown, then George Floyd and Tyre Nichols and countless others. In cities around the United States, a basic and fundamental tenet of democracy— accountability for those in charge when they failed their duty—seemed absent. We even sat spellbound as the laws governing free and fair elections nevertheless gave us someone not completely committed to democracy, arguably a narcissistic demagogue, to lead the country, though we had known for a good while that the most democratic constitutions promised liberty and equality while also producing Joseph McCarthys and Jean-Marie Le Pens.[11]

So both our political classes and the societies they represent are shattered after a tremendously challenging decade. From the Partygate scandal in the United Kingdom to the January 6 attack on the US Capitol, and others between, we wonder why our political leaders are acting so irresponsibly when the rest of us are in desperate need of good governance. Data from the World Justice Project 2022 is telling us that this is not just a subjective scholarly rant: for the fifth year in a row, the rule of law, the idea that government is bound by the same clear, consistent rules and norms it sets for us, has declined in most countries around the world.[12] And as a result of this decline and our disappointment in our leaders, we are all, more than ever, democracy's discontents, with opinion polls telling us that trust and distrust in government across much of the industrialised world are evenly felt—the same percentage of people trust government and distrust government. And that is here, in the industrialised world, with all its formal laws, where things should be a lot better than this.[13] Perhaps it is no wonder that a recent Ipsos survey showed that, on average, only 30 per cent of adults trust other people.[14]

Public intellectuals around the globe are proposing solutions to this critical mess—but their solutions come out of the same toolbox we have drawn from for centuries.[15] They are suggesting more rules to fix our broken democracies. More innovations for our political leaders. These tweaks may be helpful, indeed sometimes even necessary; but they also often amount to little more than bandages in the long run and, more often than we realise, make matters worse because we then sit back and rely on the political elites to fix things for us, to somehow succeed where they failed before.

Our constitutions and some of our laws have of course worked—they have, in some cases, provided great relief from arbitrary and brutal dictatorship, from the kind of tyranny that previous generations have known or the kind that is currently experienced by some inhabitants of the 111 countries in the world that are still rated as 'not free' or at best 'partly free' by international observers like Freedom House. In these not-free or partly free countries, individuals do not enjoy many of the basic political rights and civil liberties that we have fought to get in our 'free' spaces.[16] And to be sure, there are certainly many cases in which individual citizens, or groups of citizens, have used their laws and their constitutions to push for greater freedoms. From invoking the right to life to protecting the environment in Nepal and Montana, to using courts to safeguard access to food and reduce greenhouse gas emissions in the Netherlands and Pakistan, everyday people and interest groups are definitely calling on and using their laws and their constitutions for positive change—to better protect their rights. Certainly, laws that will regulate AI, that will protect young people from the potential harms of social media, that prohibit us from killing and abusing one another, and that deter large corporations from taking huge advantage of consumers have been and will continue to be welcome and perhaps essential legal additions, even in the vision I argue for here. There are plenty of examples of why law cannot and should not be disregarded or dissolved, and why we should not try to escape the law's limitations.

However, with law we are constantly walking a fine line between liberties, and the potential harm in their exercise. The right to bear arms, to free speech, and other so-called rights are not absolute or even widely accepted. Rights, or liberties, and the laws that protect them are contested because your freedom to do something may well interfere with my freedom, or your freedom as a member of a group (a religious or racial community) may be greater than mine, because I am not a member of that group. Think, for example, of the dispute arising during the COVID-19 pandemic, when some religious communities declared a special need to be exempt from laws prohibiting communal gatherings during lockdown; or when some public health officials defended group protests over police brutality, acknowledging that these gatherings were likely to spread COVID but demanded that they be allowed, noting that "racism also poses a dire health threat."[17] The laws and the constitution that give liberty to some must be constantly open for debate and discussion—because that liberty and its exercise do not come without potential conflicts, problems that I want to explore in detail in the pages that follow.

So one of the main tenets in this book is that it is not necessarily the laws per se that are causing the problem but the way we have relied on them to solve problems, to instruct us—the multiple ways we have used them as substitutes for our own judgement and collective action. It's a bit like writing a university essay: I remind students that we don't want to simply repeat the authors that have come before us. We use them as guides, standing on their shoulders but critically so. We lean on them to make our own arguments, rather than hiding behind them, uncritically and without thinking.

And so it is with the law. We may need and even want to lean on it from time to time, surely, but the heavy lifting needs to be done by us.

We have been clinging to a fixed point in history for a long time now, a point in which modern liberty was defined for us, not by us. This point in our history marked the end of what some philosophers believed was an awful state of nature, before any social organisation, the end of the nasty, brutish world so vividly described by political theorist Thomas Hobbes.[18] The Leviathan, our saviour, came in the form of a strong and undivided central government authority based on a contract. We had arrived, albeit through pain and suffering and a brutal war of all against all, to craft laws and even higher laws, which gave us an enduring structure and a healthy, stable order. We had arrived at liberty. We could choose our governments now, rather than have them imposed on us. We were able to enjoy many freedoms, which became understood as rights. But even if we believe in this metaphor as a useful picture of our progress, we are in a different place now. Just as we have left medieval medical practices far behind, should we not also update our idea of governing and of being governed? As Philip Morris tried to get American women to believe in the 1960s, 'You've come a long way, baby.' Yes, we have. But why should we stop here?

I am not proposing more fixes via more laws. Because I believe, now more than ever—with unprecedented technologies linking individuals, connecting the common people across the entire world—that now is the time to move outside of this inadequate box of laws and rules and hierarchical leadership, and instead make democracy work a different way. One citizen at a time.

Nevertheless, every grand funeral needs its oration, an opportunity not to praise Caesar but to bury him. To reckon with the end of constitutions as we now view them, we need a brief discussion of what law is and where it came from, why it has taken on such importance in our lives. I hope to show you why our reliance on the law to do the work of living together has become so problematic, and then show you how to engage with the solutions. What follows is a discussion of the areas I believe are key to fostering good citizenship now: leadership, fundamental rights, public spaces, food security and the environment, social diversity, and education. Here I make six interconnected suggestions that can help us become better citizens today, by helping us move away from being *subjects* and towards being *citizens*. My six ideas begin with, and are grounded in, an alternative to the idea that order is identical to stability: I ask you to instead think of order as spontaneous, self-enforcing cooperation. This is the kind of cooperation that calls for multiple leaps of faith and trust, for a way to frame our social interactions that does not rely heavily on rules and authority to dictate actions. It is transient and must be. It is contingent, and because of its contingency it may seem precarious, but think of it instead as adaptable. It is currently rare, but if it can be encouraged by stepping away from the constraint of rules, it can flourish and continually reinvent itself, providing perhaps the only social glue that will enable civilisation's discontents to get along and take care of one another.

This is, I hope to show, true citizenship. It is still membership in a state, to be sure. And as members of a state, we have a right to expect certain protections, as well as obligations to the state and its other members. But this belonging to a state involves belonging to a community of citizens, and it requires horizontal, reciprocal relationships—not just vertical ones—if it is to be real. So *citizen* here is defined in ideal terms: as a responsible, active member of the community called humanity, a member who enjoys rights but also owes obedience to herself and other humans and has an obligation to respect the rights of the earth and all its living creatures. It is an ideal and, as such, a goal. In the pages that follow, I want to remind us all how to be citizens according to this definition: horizontally, across races, across genders, across nationalities, across age groups—one simple but meaningful step at a time.

Throughout this book, I invite the reader to imagine their ideal citizen and to question their own attachment to the rules we have come to know as 'the law'. This is not a book about bad laws and good laws, or about how and why to break them; it is a book about how we have become complacent as citizens by hiding behind the law, and what we can do about it now, constructively and without violence. This is a journey we take together; it is a confession on my part as a former preacher of the law, but also a plea: for without first questioning our own attachments to rules and our reliance on laws to solve problems, without acknowledging our own fears about what a world beyond laws might look like, we will never allow our minds to travel in that important imaginative direction that can enable us to envision an alternative world. Let us begin this together and see just how far we can go.

CHAPTER ONE

Lessons from the Law

THERE IS A SMALL VOLCANIC ISLAND, REMOTE IN both time and space, that I think can help us understand why rules are part of the problem. It is a place of sensual beauty, surrounded by a coral reef, the air scented by baobab fruit and ylang-ylang. Lost in the Mozambique Channel, so tiny, and perhaps to some so insignificant, a set of islands known as Mayotte nevertheless serves as an important microcosm of the contemporary world.

On a blistering July afternoon in 2005, I arrived, malarial and unveiled, on this island during my summer break from teaching, intending to study the version of Islamic law practised here since the seventh century. Hakim, the grand qadi of Mayotte and the highest religious authority on the island, welcomed me into his courtroom. It was here, as Hakim explained this mysterious place, in a colourful breeze-block building adjacent to the mosque, that I began to think profoundly about what law *really* was.

We began with the Qur'an, one of the sacred texts that guides Islamic judges such as Hakim in their decision making. According to the holy book, Allah gave order to the universe by calling the earth and sky to come together in obedience to him: the earth and sky, not man, were first made subjects of Allah and depended upon his authority for a good and safe cosmic order. Authority, and everyone's and everything's obedience to it, were born. Almost all religious traditions, including my own, share a similar creation story. Take, for example, the book of Genesis, sacred to Jewish and Christian peoples, where we are told that God created the universe in a precise and good order out of nothing:

And God said, Let there be light. . . .

And God made the two great lights; the greater light to rule the day, and the lesser light to rule the night: He made the stars also.

And God set them in the firmament of heaven to
give light upon the earth, and to rule over the day
and over the night, and to divide the light from
the darkness: and God saw that it was good.

Indeed, in the Abrahamic religions, including the one in which I was raised, this precise and good order created by God was to last through all generations. But of course, order would then require the obedience of the original couple, Adam and Eve, and their compliance with God's authority. In many countries of the world today, it is this narrative that is embedded in our social fabric: in our families, our communities, and our leaders. It infuses and gives shape to them.

Other creation myths in different parts of the world are based on a conception of the world before the divine order as terrible chaos rather than nothingness. Some Korean narratives tell this story, for example, with complex, combined influences of the various faiths that have been important to Korea's history, including Confucianism and Buddhism, Shamanism and Christianity, in multiple and subtle variations.[1]

These creation myths, in spite of their differences, each claim that the order of the universe that came after divine intervention is both good and requires authority. Other myths from other cultures, including some Meso-American narratives, also inculcate an attachment to order and authority, but the good order comes about when authority in the form of gods destroys what was considered problematic and then recreates what is not.[2]

Back in the biblical Garden of Eden, through their mere humanity, their curiosity and hunger for knowledge, Adam and Eve blew it, spoiled the good original order, resulting in humanity's eternal search to restore God's 'good' order and open the door to salvation. Fortunately, God made it a bit easier, for he gave future generations their first principles, or standards of behaviour, which then became written rules, to help this process: Obey only me. Do not kill. Do not steal. Et cetera. These rules had and continue to have important functions in societies and communities around the world. But the problem just might be that they were also used as the origin of our modern secular laws and the basis, eventually, of our constitutions. We were told how to behave, how to do the right thing. So Secular Fallacy No. 1 was born: nature needs authority for good order to exist.

All these rules were apparently necessary, especially as our families grew larger, our tribes grew into communities, and our contact with others expanded. Rules were a good start at stable order, at helping us escape the constant conflict and disagreement that were inherent in human nature. And they were also a start of an imposed predictable order, not an emergent one. But by now being articulated as rules rather than guiding principles, and by being imposed by some authority, they also suggested, ironically, that left to our own devices, we would steal, we would kill, we would behave like savages in the state of nature. Rules were the answer to the perceived disorder of nature. And so Secular Fallacy No. 2 was born: what is good about this good order is that it is imposed by an authority and is actually *stable*.

Eventually, our populations grew larger, and they grew much faster than our resources did. Now we needed something more, something bigger and better: we needed something to keep our emerging societies safe, stable of course, and predictable—because predictability helps keep things stable. We needed something that tied us into our group and allowed members of the group to get along primarily with each other, while keeping others out. We needed something that carried with it a form of consequence when the rules keeping stable order were broken. That something was law.

Law, in its most basic form, is defined simply as a rule, code, or other formal system that is enforced through some institution. Legal historians tell us that law, understood this way, had its origins in the development of civilisation—of complex societies, such as that of ancient Egypt, dating as far back as 3000 BC.[3] Legal anthropologists tell us that law, understood similarly but without restricting the idea to a code or any formal system, had its origins in almost any of the social groups that emerged throughout history and used rules and consequences to achieve social harmony.[4] And some, but not all, legal philosophers tell us that a law can be distinguished from a principle—the latter is a standard we are expected to observe because it is a requirement of justice, or fairness, or morality, and one that can be more or less important in a given circumstance, whereas a law is either valid or it is not.[5]

So modern law as we know it today in our advanced industrial democracies is at its most basic form a humanly devised constraint that is tied to authority and that also allows this authority to punish those who break it.[6] It works through reward (inclusion in the community, with the benefits of membership) and punishment (exclusion from the community, in some cases imprisonment or death). Law, and its partner law enforcement, have developed through time to provide the basis for order as we want it to be: stable, predictable, and controllable from above. We still embrace this, unquestioningly, today, living in groups with a single hierarchical authority over us, co-creating a single, and artificially fixed, physical space: a nation-state.

There are numerous areas of our lives governed by specific laws, such as family law, criminal law, tax law, environmental law, and water law. There is even an emerging area known as space law, as we continue to expand and as our world thinks increasingly about other worlds beyond our own. And an equally emerging field of animal law, as people begin to think more systematically about the rights other animals have, to be treated with the respect we each demand for ourselves.

Most of these laws can be and are altered over time. They are often made by a local authority, by the governors on behalf of the governed. Local laws for local people.

The highest form of law, of this humanly devised constraint, is a constitution. It is a set of principles which sets up a governing structure for a people, providing a framework for how they are meant to interact with one another, and for what purposes. This higher law is expected to outlast other laws, and so it is deliberately hard to change once established. Nor is it made by local councils or parliaments but by an exceptional authority at a national level. Likewise, it sits above all other laws. It is the framework for all groups and communities living within the borders of the nation-state, the framework against which that nation-state's other laws can be judged and to which those other laws must conform. The constitution is the foundation and the roof, the entire house, within which all the members of the nation-state—the citizens—and the government of the nation-state coexist, and within which all other laws and rules function. It is sometimes understood, too, as a contract between the governed and the governors, between those we place in power through elections to manage the household and the rest of us: we the people, the citizens who live in it. Our constitutional contract tells both sides—us and them—what we and they can and cannot do, and what we and they can and cannot expect from one another. The constitutional contract provides a roof of rights over our heads. It sets guidelines for defining our borders. It sets our values. It tells us how our leaders will be chosen, and how we can get rid of them if they perform badly. It is the ultimate form of order making in a democracy, and every democratic country in the world has one; whether codified in a single, ratified document or not—every democracy has a constitution. By establishing this stable legal order over the entire territory and setting up our fundamental rights and obligations through it, our Secular Fallacy No. 3 was born: constitutions give us a just order—and, protecting it, constitutions give us justice.

Our earliest forms of what we think of as a constitution, our proto-constitutions, emerged in antiquity, as people sought to establish peaceful and self-contained communities, with forms of government and authority to protect these communities from outside threats.[7]

Athens was one such place, and Aristotle was one of the first to think through the idea of a constitution as higher law, as a foundation for stable political order, and as something that should not be easy to change at whim. With Aristotle, we began to understand that a constitution could be a blueprint for life as a member of a community, such as a city-state. In antiquity, this blueprint was the set of laws that told us who was a free man and a citizen and who was a slave. And so even in its nascent form, one critical purpose of a constitution was to set out the rules for a just order—for justice. Rome was another place where the idea of a higher law started to form, to provide not only a law of the land but a blueprint for life in the community. There were marked differences in the way these different ancients conceived of and practised what we now refer to as constitutionalism, but both saw the need for an overarching framework, tied to an idea of justice.

In many other parts of the world, similar proto-constitutions were established, from Mesopotamia to India to Asia. And in England, perhaps most famously, King John was persuaded to sign the English version of a proto-constitution in 1215—the Magna Carta—spelling out a just order that prevented any king from punishing or excluding anyone from the community without due process of law. Such predictable, non-arbitrary order entrusted peace to a central authority and told us right from wrong.

That particular moment is hailed as one of the most important moments in the development of constitutions, but also in the development of ordinary rules and laws—for it is a turning point at which modern liberty is defined. And this trend continued, with constitutions being crafted at various points over the next centuries, with countries from France, the Netherlands, and the United States, to Poland and Haiti and Bavaria in Germany, among others, all drafting documents that looked like and were considered versions of higher law. In the early to middle 1800s, North America, Latin America and the Caribbean, and western Europe saw some of the first codified documents, to be followed in the early 1900s with the start of codified constitutions in the Middle East, North Africa, and eastern Europe; and Asia and sub-Saharan Africa some decades later.[8]

But . . . were there other possibilities, other competing ideas that might have taken us in a different direction?

Certainly there were. One subtly, but critically, different possibility was suggested by Roman lawyer and statesman Marcus Tullius Cicero. Cicero did believe in authority and rules, but as complements to an all-important idea he referred to as 'attitude'. That's right, having a bad attitude for Cicero was a thing. His *De officiis*, the book of advice or 'obligations' he offered to young Romans, encourages behaviour not only via rules but often also by appealing to an idea of the collective, of fellowship in humanity. Cicero eloquently calls for much of what we have since forgotten; for example, in Book 3 of this great work, he emphasises that 'we must all adhere to the principle that what is useful to the individual is identical with what is useful to the community. . . . [A]s for those who argue that we must take sympathetic account of fellow-citizens but not of outsiders, they are destroying the fellowship common to the human race, and once this is removed, kindness, generosity, goodness and justice are wholly excluded.'[9] These conceptions of community and of justice are not mere platitudes, because Roman law was generally influenced by many such ideas and values aimed at encouraging a shared feeling of a collective that also went beyond the immediate community, rather than the individual autonomy that has been encouraged in our current laws and even formed the basis of some of our constitutions.

Reinhard Zimmermann, an important scholar of Roman law, states it clearly for us in his explanation of ancient Rome, where 'individualism never reigned supreme. *Fides, amicitia, pietas, humanitas* and *officium* have repeatedly been referred to: they created a value system and a specific kind of social ethics determining the behavior of the (upper-class) Roman citizen. Individualism was not his social ideal; on the contrary: he felt obliged to help his friends. . . . All this was part of the *officium amici*, and it could matter little whether such help had been specifically solicited or not.'[10]

Think how different this is from the contemporary American idea of the citizen, vividly parodied in an episode of the sitcom *Seinfeld*.[11] Jerry Seinfeld and his friends, while visiting a suburban town, joke and laugh as they watch a stranger being robbed. When a police officer spots them, he arrests them for criminal indifference. Shocked and confused, they contact a lawyer, who reassures them that the police officer is wrong, that in the United States you 'don't have to help anybody. That's what this country is all about.' Later in court, this lawyer (played by the brilliant Phil Morris) argues on their behalf: 'Bystanders are by definition innocent!' he emphatically claims. 'But no, they [the police] want to change nature, they want to create a whole new animal. The Guilty Bystander!' Indeed, this is exactly what some Romans intended to do.

So seeds for a different possibility, for law that encouraged and was firmly grounded in both a sense of the collective and of humanity more generally, were definitely there. But eventually, this humane conception of the common good, and the inculcation of a kind of civic virtue that it was designed for, lost out in many places to the idea and practice of both individualism and its twin, the giving over of responsibility to a powerful state, with its machinery in the form of an army and the police. Not only did this different idea of the engaged citizen—one who would not be welcomed into the community if he remained a guilty bystander—lose out, but in some notable places it was even mocked.

In the period we refer to as early modern Europe, between the Middle Ages and the Industrial Revolution, wars broke out repeatedly between various factions on a continent that was still trying to define its peoples and decide their borders. In the same period, from the end of the fifteenth through to the end of the eighteenth century, revolutionary ideas of freedom and equality spread throughout these lands, fuelling new conceptions of government—challenging those that had been based on the privileges that came with certain class ties, being born into certain families, or having connections with the church. These were important ways of thinking about our horizontal ties to each other, to fellow citizens. But at the same time, with the rise, for example, of Napoleon in France and his occupation of Italy, thoughts of hierarchy and unification, of a central and strong authority reigning and bringing together the different peoples living in one land, also started to take root. The peoples of this Europe began to see the attraction and merit of a more consensual kind of rule, call it a more democratic form of rule, but also of a 'united we stand' approach to community. We began entrusting state builders with our hard-earned money to carve roads, build schools, and train armies—with all the things that would bring and keep us closer together and protect us from outside savages. We acquiesced in this development because it felt safer and more progressive. In many ways, it was. It *was* development. But the problem is that we also acquiesced in it because it was practical and so much easier than doing the heavy lifting ourselves.

There were certainly some who still worried about leaving this heavy lifting to authority and the law, like the nineteenth-century French philosopher and politician Pierre-Joseph Proudhon, who had a strong suspicion of the law and the kind of order it established. Proudhon advocated a society that could exist without the constraint of authority, warning that 'to be governed is to be kept in sight, inspected, spied upon, directed, law-driven, numbered, enrolled, indoctrinated, preached at, controlled, estimated, valued, censured, commanded, by creatures who have neither the right, nor the wisdom, nor the virtue to do so . . . '.[12] Considered by some the father of modern anarchy, he knew the system from the inside, as a politician himself, and he hoped for something better than what he was experiencing first-hand.

Similarly, some economists from the Scottish Enlightenment and their followers, like Michael Polanyi, remained concerned about the increasing over-regulation of our lives in this modern state and instead argued that spontaneous cooperation, even if it were based on self-interest, was the best precursor to a thriving society.[13] Polanyi believed that the end result of authority was a kind of order, yes, but one that approached paralysis. So he cautioned that if we are interested in good order, which he considered spontaneous order, we did not want any single authority organising us from above, and certainly not from some arbitrary centre.

Perhaps the earliest recorded call for spontaneous cooperation in lieu of order by a central authority that I am aware of was by the Chinese philosopher Chuang Tzu.[14] Writing in the fourth century BC, this father of Taoism hoped for the possibility of emergent order. He urged continual, spontaneous action and reaction to life, rather than the careful planning of it. Not only was it possible to let things alone to develop along their own path; it was necessary. The early call for less orderly order was already there.

While these theorists had limits and were obviously theorising in times very different from our own, the core of what they noticed and found troubling is real and very present today. The hesitations they expressed and the alternatives they offered lost out to the idea of order as stability, conceived of as a body of laws, rules, and, ultimately, constitutions—rooted in creation myths, based on hierarchy and central authority, and made to be anything but flexible or spontaneous.

When we now look back at the past couple of centuries of constitution making, we can see a pattern in the way constitutions were crafted and animated by what I am going to call 'hopes', or guiding principles. And two rather distinct patterns emerge. First, in some constitutions, the animating hopes were something like the life, liberty, and the pursuit of happiness of the US Declaration of Independence, and this is perhaps most obviously seen in the American Constitution with its focus on the individual.[15] In other constitutions, particularly the post–Second World War documents, the animating hope of the constitutional document and its design was something very different: human dignity. This difference is an important one, because the motivational hopes of constitutional democracy as expressed in these constitutions actually became alternate sets of first principles for their designs—and for the architecture of rights. The first set, what might also be called the Franco-American pattern, considered life, liberty, and the pursuit of happiness to be the fundamental revolutionary and republican 'hopes', guiding design, separation-of-powers agreements, and other institutional arrangements, as well as the nature and scope of popular sovereignty. This structure is rather different from the postwar German model, which also inspired the South

African constitution and some of the recent eastern European constitutions, for which human dignity becomes the fundamental guiding principle and animating hope, the highest value of higher law, the most inalienable part of 'their law', with powerful constitutional courts carved into that stone to protect this value, above all.

What we have to ask ourselves very honestly is, stepping back from the documents and their animating hopes, Did we achieve life, liberty, and the pursuit of happiness? Is our dignity better protected, and do we protect the dignity of others? Have either of these patterns helped us achieve our hopes—those that animated our constitutions in the first place? To be sure, there were great achievements in life and liberty as well as dignity in these times. Arbitrary power was limited, freedom of religion and speech guaranteed. It is far from perfect, but then again, some will argue that these are aspirational, and when understood that way, yes, they are doing their job as we strive to ensure in our imperfect human world that we try our best to come as close as we can to the ideals.[16]

But I'm not sure that we have either come far enough along or that the gains we have made are owed to our constitutions. And I'm not sure that these documents have done that much to help us be better citizens.

Now, this might have been a quick and dirty version of constitutional history. But it is, I promise you, a pretty accurate one. My point here is not to provide you with a meticulous causal history of global law and constitutional thought. Rather, I am offering what the sociologist Charles Tilly might have called a 'superior story', a story that is certainly consistent with the full, adequate accounts of history but is meant to enlighten and clarify, rather than detail all the mechanisms and processes.[17] My essential point instead is that, as I explore in the six solutions that follow, the secular fallacies that we based our laws on made us believe that we would have good, stable order if we set up our societies through a hierarchy of laws and a belief in leadership. But what I want to show in the following chapters is how our reliance on these secular fallacies actually withered our ability to do democracy well. To get this, we need to remember that law is an artificial construct, a mere parameter marking acceptable behaviour. A constitution is the highest form of law and so, the highest form of this artificiality. It is the set of rules that organises a state and guides interactions between us all. Directly or through interpretation, it tells us which people can legally have intercourse in the privacy of their own homes, whether they can marry and enjoy the financial protection of the state. It tells us whether we can legally own weapons. Whether we can help someone in deep pain end their life. Whether a woman has a right to abort a foetus. It tells us all these things. Or tries to. Sometimes it does not. Most often, as I explore below, it tells us very ambiguously.

Most ordinary law comes about through proposals that originate either in the legislature, or in another area of government, or with an interest group or even an individual. In the best of cases, government and interested groups discuss drafts of the idea, which, if it is successful enough to make it to the status of a bill—a proposed law—it will be debated, and people with relevant expertise will be invited to give opinions on the merits, or drawbacks, of the proposed law. Eventually, if the idea makes it this far, it is put to a vote—a vote of the legislature, or of the legislature and an upper house, if it exists. Or a public vote. Or perhaps even a combination of these things. The law that eventually emerges will ideally have been formed through many iterations among many bodies, including committees which sometimes include members of the public. The more bodies involved in the actual voting, the more 'veto points'—opportunities for the proposed law to be altered, axed, or substituted by a counter-proposal. As political scientist Ellen Immergut said, 'By envisioning political systems as sets of interconnected arenas and examining the rules of representation within each, one can predict where such "veto points" are likely to arise.'[18] It is perhaps for this reason that when ABC television in the United States decades ago showed brief educational cartoons between children's programming, the one explaining American government's executive, legislative, and judicial branches, and their role in law making, described it as a 'three-ring circus'.[19] Or take the line that has been attributed to Mark Twain and Otto von Bismarck, among others: 'People who love sausage and respect the law should never watch either one being made.'[20] This is the messy reality of law making when it is done democratically and even if it is done well.

So now what? If this story is all to be believed, if the way we make our laws is messy and in some sense unpredictable at the best of times, and if the highest form of our law is at best ambiguous and wide open to interpretation, what anchor do we have for our democracies, for our societies? Do we simply accept our broken democracies, our failed policies, and seemingly rudderless societies, and just keep working to try to make the rules better? Do we subscribe to anarchy? It is often said, after all, that democracy is simply the least bad of all the other forms of government and still a lot less problematic than mob rule. But is that enough? Or do we try something else, something that is radically different from both extremes?

One late summer afternoon, back in my current hometown, Oxford, I stood in a playground, thinking about all of this, watching my son work together with other children, strangers all of them, at a water pump, to solve a problem, without any one of them, or any adult, telling the others what to do: heretical ideas on obedience and democracy were born. I suddenly wondered, what if we had gone the other way, with Cicero, Tzu, and the different drummers? What if we came together when it was necessary to unblock the water pumps, to help solve problems, spontaneously and without waiting for authority? What if this was our way of understanding what it meant to be a good citizen, a good bystander?

Rules, and especially laws, are a surrogate, at best, for real order: for the spontaneous type of order that comes when ordinary people like you and me and the woman next to us on the bus care enough about something to make it work for everyone involved, without any authority or rule on top. Self-enforcing local commitment and cooperation cannot develop, cannot flourish, if the rules and courts are asked to do the work for us. Because they can't. *We* must. So how?

Part II

THE SOLUTIONS

CHAPTER TWO

Don't Play Follow the Leader

I N 2017, TWO SIMPLE PRINCIPLES—EMPATHY AND solidarity—came together through a virtual, decentralised movement to topple one of Hollywood's most elusive and powerful sexual predators: Harvey Weinstein. Igniting a process that would bring a form of justice for his victims, the #MeToo hashtag then exploded into a phenomenon, making it possible, through the incremental movements of thousands of individuals who shared painful stories of abuse, to cause a global change in the way we think about consent, authority, and power. The butterfly effect happened before our eyes: small changes, locally, resulted in very big changes, globally.[1] And the world, its citizens and its governments, had to listen this time.

One of the main problems with laws, and in particular our modern constitutions, is their focus on centralised, hierarchical leadership—elements that are at the very least orthogonal to, if not countervailing forces against, the decentralised, non-hierarchical processes of #MeToo and other important social movements that have made substantial improvements in the way we enjoy our rights and treat others. It makes sense, historically, for law to be this way, because proto-constitutions such as the Magna Carta originated from a need to control absolute leadership and regulate it, limiting it to make it less arbitrary. So our modern constitutions and electoral laws tell us that the leader, the chief executive, will be the one with the most votes—an absolute majority, or a plurality, or whatever the electoral law states. That leader may win by only a small margin of votes to get to the required majority or plurality, and yet they, or their party, goes on to represent and lead all members of that polity, usually a diverse set of peoples, and often for a fixed number of years. There was and continues to be an important debate in constitutional law and political science on the institution of the presidency, the role of the prime minister, the relative merits and drawbacks of presidential and parliamentary systems. Particularly in the wake of violence surrounding presidential leadership contests in the United States and Brazil or scandals surrounding parliamentary leadership in the United Kingdom and Germany, more of us are beginning to question whether the Magna Carta and its successors can still do the job they were intended to do, if they ever could: providing control over those who govern us and fostering the kind of responsible, respectable leadership worthy of our allegiance.

Almost every democracy in the world with a constitution has had problems, at some point, with leadership: corruption, as in Austria in 2021; extremism, as in Italy in 2023; inability to get along constructively and respectfully with an opponent, as in the United States under Donald Trump's administration. There have been scandals over all sorts of misconduct, from lying to sexual offences to financial improprieties, as well as what seems like constant incendiary rhetoric, at least in some democracies, where leaders blame each other publicly for the woes of the country, when they should instead be demonstrating exemplary attitudes of respect and cooperation as part of their mandate to 'lead' their people.

When I first advised governments on constitutional choice, for example, addressing former presidents and prime ministers from around the world at the Club of Madrid, I was part of a group of scholars that went around suggesting our presidential systems were particularly problematic because of the rule structure inherent in the constitution. Parliamentary constitutions, like Germany or Italy, had a head of government who needed the support of parliament to get into office and stay there, to get policies into place, to govern. An unpopular prime minister could be voted out of office with enough pressure from the parliament and a no-confidence motion. This, we argued, gave prime ministers more incentives to bargain with parliament and compromise over policies in order to survive, and correspondingly we found that bargaining and compromise happened in parliamentary systems more than it did under presidential constitutions. It had to. In the presidential system, the head of government is not someone who comes to office indirectly after their political party wins the most votes in a national election. Instead, the head of state is directly elected by the people separately from the elections to the legislature, so there are fewer incentives for cooperation from the start. The presidential and legislative terms are fixed and independent of each other, and new election dates are known well in advance.

So it was for us back then the *kind* of rule that was the problem, not *all* the rules. That might still be the case. The presidential system, with its fixed electoral terms and its separate mandates for the executive and legislative branches of power, actually structures gridlock and division and the kind of impasse on policy that if you have an army and a history of military involvement in politics, is more likely than a parliamentary system to wind up in a coup or, as we have seen in the United States or more recently in Brazil, an insurrection. But is the parliamentary constitution much better, really? Take the United Kingdom, a parliamentary system with an uncodified constitution—a constitution made up of not one single document but of a substantial collection of relevant statutes that have existed for the past eight hundred years or so. Proponents of the parliamentary system will tell you that, in spite of the many challenges that have arisen over the postwar decades, the UK has never seen a coup or an American-style insurrection, because an unpopular prime minister simply loses support in parliament and has no choice but to seek support agreements from other parties or step down. But the lack of violence in this process does not mean that the United Kingdom is a higher-quality democracy, that it is well governed, or that its leadership enjoys broad legitimacy. Just look at Boris Johnson's performance during the COVID-19 pandemic, the Partygate affair, the sex scandal involving his ministers, the behaviour of the police forces and other institutions during this period, and then the quick succession of prime ministers after he eventually, and reluctantly, stepped down. Markets were thrown into turmoil and his successor lasted less than a couple of months before Johnson and other members of the Conservative Party threw their hats back into the bitter race. Is that good enough? Policy and leadership during this period may not have looked as bad as it did on Capitol Hill, but it certainly did not prevent police brutality or deaths from COVID; so do the rules prove better than across the pond, where presidential constitutions are encouraging more violent power struggles? Is this the best we can do?

By following all these rules and trusting in them to yield the right outcome, we forget along the way to ask ourselves whether emerging leaders are really and truly worthy of our allegiance, even if all the rules were followed; or whether, like a problematic algorithm showing us ads for something we have no interest in buying, the process and all the rules have, in aggregate, privileged a bad mistake.

What's the alternative to leadership in a democracy or even to the electoral laws that tell us how to get our leaders? Spontaneous, horizontal, non-hierarchical self-sufficiency. And we have just witnessed some very important examples of good democratic organising: spontaneous, non-hierarchical order during the pandemic of 2019–2021 which worked in the real world, and did so when leaders were failing us in the midst of an insurrection, arguably instigated by the outgoing president himself, in one of the most important democracies in the world. Those examples showed us, for the most part, emergent, constructive order. In fact, when many governments and their structures failed us acutely over the past years, we quickly and effectively acted ourselves, locally but with mirror movements globally, all without waiting for hierarchical leadership to instruct us. Outside of and despite government, both the post-Occupy social justice movement and the mutual aid societies that sprang up in the face of the pandemic demonstrated that we can and will seek what we consider just. We will, under the right conditions, make the right order. Black Lives Matter used spontaneous protest, aided by social media networks, to invigorate and encourage a young generation of activists who united around a common goal. COVID-19 mutual aid societies took to the streets, carefully delivering food and medicine to quarantined people while their governments were still bickering over the importance of face masks. Both demonstrate that we have the moral fibre to live without stable order and without blindly following leaders, and to live together well. Or, at least as well as if we left it all up to our government.

A few years ago, in the French city of Grenoble, in a housing project known as Villanueva, at the base of the French Alps, a group of strangers came together spontaneously in an urban housing block to save two young brothers from a burning apartment. The boys, aged three and ten, were trapped nearly fifty feet above the ground. Seven men, immigrants from various former French colonies, heard the boys' screams and came together outside the block. None of them knew the others. But without hesitating, they quickly organised themselves, interlocking arms and shouting at the boys to jump. The majority of these seven men were injured by the rescue, several needing surgeries; the boys' fall broke some of the rescuers' arms, fingers, and even shoulders. But the boys went

unscathed. Later that year, the mayor's office held a ceremony to publicly thank these men for their altruism. Only
six of the seven received awards. The seventh man was an
undocumented migrant, who fled quickly after his critical
part in the rescue. He had risked not only broken bones
but his freedom to help those boys, and then he ran away
from the law.[2]

Now that may be a very small-scale, in-the-moment
example. But it shares qualities with the altruism and
action of neighbours during Hurricane Katrina in New
Orleans in 2005 or that of ordinary Californians during
the San Francisco Earthquake in 1906. Or let's go back
a decade, to the wave of protests that emerged in one of
the last green spaces and public spheres in the increasingly
built-up city of Istanbul. In 2013, government plans to
appropriate this space for a shopping mall sparked community action, which blossomed into protests that eventually spread to the rest of Turkey. Known as the Gezi
Park movement, the subsequent nationwide protests have
been compared to the protests of May '68 and Occupy.
As Zeynep Tufekci describes in one of her accounts, 'The
Gezi Park protests, like many other protests around the
world, favored self-organization and rejected formal politics and organizations. Volunteers ran everything, including communal kitchens, libraries, and clinics that cared
both for protestors with minor ailments and those with
life-threatening injuries.'[3] This is spontaneous, horizontal,
non-hierarchical self-sufficiency, focused on a particular

issue or set of grievances. It is often provoked, or inspired, by some immediate need, a governmental action or inaction that leaves a vacuum—a chasm between what is being supplied and what citizens want or need. The examples are reminiscent in some ways of the shadow economies that sprang up in the centrally planned economies of the Soviet bloc, with the key difference, of course, that unlike shadow economies under communism, these movements and their economies are not working towards surreptitious private gain but rather towards recognition for very public community goals. Sometimes they get them. In 2012, Andrew Haldane, a representative of the Bank of England, publicly stated that the Occupy movement protesting inequality was both morally and intellectually right in its claims about the international financial system. In 2014, the Los Angeles City Council passed a resolution to support the Occupy movement in LA and embraced some of its concerns and its goals.[4] A conversation between self-organised citizens and local government began.

This may seem very modern, as social media has featured so prominently in the story of Occupy and other movements. Some of this self-organised self-help has certainly made use of social media to organise and coalesce, but some has not. It is not in fact a prerequisite, and those without access to the internet or apps on their phones have and do manage to self-organise.[5] Take the regular Monday demonstrations in Leipzig, East Germany, in the 1980s, in which a small number of demonstrators first made it known locally that they would get together on that day in a specific part of the city to protest the socialist government and Erich Honecker's authoritarian rule. Creating what has been called an 'information cascade' by behavioural economists, the protestors made it possible for ordinary citizens to physically see the mounting dissatisfaction with the regime, as each week the number of protestors grew. They could share information about the precarious political and economic state of the country and the regime more generally, questioning the propaganda spread by the East German and Soviet governments, and public opinion gradually mounted against the regime, culminating in the fall of the Berlin Wall.[6]

So what is it about spontaneous cooperation that we can learn from and try to inculcate as a default behaviour, rather than an extreme one in extreme times? All these examples share five elements. First, people recognise a common, concrete need, a vacuum to be filled. Second, this need is made known, and people act on it, often by spreading accurate, first-hand information. Third, those acting are doing so for the sake of this need, which is in some way a shared one, a shared stress. Fourth, any imminent danger or metaphorical evil or its cause is seen as emanating from outside the immediate community—it is external. And fifth, a mini-economy of self-organised individuals develops around this need to support the heavy lifting that needs to be done.[7]

A little more detail can help us pull out some lessons. Charles Fritz, an American soldier stationed in Bath, England, during the Second World War, observed with great curiosity and anthropological attention the behaviour of his proximate social circles during the war, for in spite of the general sense of fear and deprivation across the world at this time, people in his immediate surroundings seemed hopeful and relatively happy. He was struck by the fact that 'the traditional British class distinctions had largely disappeared. People who had never spoken to each other before the war, now engaged in warm, caring personal relations; they spoke openly with one another about their cares, fears, and hopes; and they gladly shared their scarce supplies with others who had greater needs. Despite the fact that American and other Allied servicemen might have been resented for adding more competition for scarce resources, they were warmly welcomed into British homes, where they found a home-away-from-home atmosphere that assuaged their loneliness for their own home and family.'[8] Later, returning to the United States to study sociology at the University of Chicago, Fritz went on to publish some of the most fascinating work on disaster and its relevance for everyday life, detailing what he called the 'therapeutic effects of disaster' and thinking through ways that we could, we should, harness the great surge in altruistic and pro-social behaviour that comes from disaster and use it to make a sustained contribution to our social lives.[9]

What did his research find? There was little in there about rules and laws. If we think about it, rules and laws are some of the first things to be suspended in times of emergency. In a previous life, this would have caused panic in me, for when rules and rights are suspended in the name of 'emergency' and 'public order', governments can and sometimes do take advantage of this space to push controversial agendas.[10] But what Fritz found was that, whatever governments might be doing during those times, everyday citizens' aggression towards others, as well as our aggression towards ourselves, did not increase, at least not during disasters. It decreased. In addition, Fritz's somewhat counter-intuitive findings showed that disasters were often followed by an immediate high morale among communities that had been victims, as a desire for a rapid return to normal spread throughout the community. What seems most important for us is that Fritz believed there were concrete ways to use this innate human tendency towards constructive, cooperative behaviour and turn it into something, well, let's call it 'everyday'. The 'therapeutic' elements of temporary disaster societies, as he called it, made for more lasting, quotidian cornerstones of our communities.

Disasters galvanise people and promote altruistic behaviour unlike other types of stress that people face. Natural disasters are both concrete (an earthquake, a pandemic, a tsunami are visible and measurable) rather than vague and abstract, and they are perceived as being outside acts, acts of some almost supernatural origin, rather than human acts that are both internal to the community and humanly devised. This combination makes disasters very different from the tensions of everyday life and from the threats to our security and safety that come from racism, homophobia, and other divisions and tensions inside our societies. They are the big, quantifiable external monsters, rather than the amorphous internal ones. That does not mean we can't change our response to the amorphous, internal ones. First, we have to take steps to flip the monsters: begin by acknowledging everyday stress as shared stress, a kind of 'we are all in this together' belief. The death of a loved one, a divorce, the adoption of a child— these are in our modern industrial societies deeply private affairs. While most media encourage private mindfulness and de-stressing to be done in the privacy of our homes, I wonder about encouraging the opposite: dramatising the stress experienced by one member of our community as a shared event. If my six-year-old daughter tells me that her schoolmate is about to lose his father to a terminal illness, what can we, as a community of parents, teachers, and children, do to share the stress of this tragedy? How can we allow space for both the privacy and dignity of the immediate family, the intimacy of the last precious moments they have together, and also collectively mourn the loss and share the stress of that father's absence, as a community? This does sometimes happen, to some extent, in some cultures, but not often enough. And we must also work hard to acknowledge the everyday stress of racism, misogyny, and other wrongs as *public* wrongs, not only against some of us but as wrongs against all of us, as insults to the community as a whole.

Why? Because what research shows us is that communities that looked after one another historically, and not just during disasters, were also those communities that shared stress regularly, that made the punctuated attacks on an individual's wellbeing an assault against the public, and not just private, life.[11] Changes induced by a trauma are easier to accept and process when widely shared, as in disaster situations, and the communities that share those pains are more robust and resilient. If modern life has meant that we keep our own traumas private, it has also meant that the frustration and traumas of everyday life remains within us as individuals and so becomes isolating and divisive. Such isolation and division return us to the Hobbesian world of all against all that our rules and laws and constitutions were meant to fix in the first place. No wonder they don't work to encourage altruism and community and fight division and isolation. Because in trying to offer us a Leviathan, these laws and constitutions took away what we probably most needed: shared experience and shared responsibility.

Scholars have wondered about how shared crisis can affect long-standing social divisions, not just those of class, as Fritz saw, but also racial and ethnic ones. They have documented something fascinating: that shared losses, such as those during natural disasters, inspired transcendent goals, so people had a reason to come together and work together even if it meant crossing some invisible lines. Divisions by class, ethnicity, and hierarchy were, at least temporarily, bridged during this process—and this led to temporary utopias, where people came together to, quite simply, help one another, regardless of previous attachments to mutually exclusive groups. Now these divisions are not easily erased, and I don't pretend that among the countless countries with deep divisions, those that have also suffered natural disasters have magically come out of the rubble on top. But natural disasters strike all and do not discriminate. Their effects disproportionately affect those whose infrastructure is less well built, to be sure, which often has something to do with class and race. This can be and often is polarising. But there is nevertheless a sense of shared destruction by an outside, random event, and by externalising that destruction and emphasising that it was not caused by a member of the community and acknowledging that it has affected and flattened everyone's world, it might just offer the kind of unstructured social landscape that is, quite literally, a tabula rasa, with new possibilities, new opportunities for innovation, cooperation, and change.

The relevance and possibility of Fritz's and others' work was examined some decades later by Rebecca Solnit, whose own accounts of 'paradise built in hell' offered inspirational stories of solidarity, mutual aid, and genuine civil-society-in-action during disasters as diverse as the Blitz in 1940s London and the 1985 Mexico City Earthquake—countering the prevailing suggestion that crises are always followed by looting and only the most selfish acts. She poignantly concludes her work claiming that the individuals and organisations that she researched for her book are able to act because they are 'motivated by hope and by love rather than fear. They are akin to a shadow government—another system ready to do more were they voted into power. Disaster votes them in. . . . Disaster reveals what else the world could be like.'[12]

We *can* get the world to look this good now, like it does during acute disasters, without the destruction that disaster brings to communities and lives but with the destruction that it brings to our fears and alienation, to our class and racial and ethnic walls, to our deep privatisation of life and to our inward-looking gaze. Make no mistake, privacy is and should be central to our rights and to our obligations to others. We all have, as human beings, the 'right to be let alone'.[13] But when we remain so attached to privacy that we bury ourselves deeply within it and use it as a wedge between us and the community, privacy itself becomes problematic and distorted.

We can start by sharing stress, as a threat to all of us. Even if we are selfish, we know that poverty within our immediate community leads to negative externalities which are problematic for all—not just the poor. Poverty raises crime rates, increases health expenditures, and so affects all of us. But beyond this selfish point of view, we must also feel compassion for the poor among us. This is sharing the stress and making the evil external so that we are better able to find a solution to it.

And we can then move to organising around immediate needs, for there may not always be crises, thankfully, but there will always be needs. Case in point: State schools in some countries have been offering government-subsidised school meals, so that children can be guaranteed at least one nutritionally balanced meal per day during the school week. But delays in legislation often affect the distribution of these meals. As one example, recently in Scotland, government ministers and teachers locked horns over the provision, noting that free school meals needed to be extended to all primary school pupils.[14] These debates engender delays and blame games, not just in Scotland but in countries around the world, because they are political— not everyone agrees that we need to spend taxpayers' money to feed children. And, consequently, policy in this area tends to be haphazardly implemented, even though we know how important these meals are to the developing future minds of our countries. Recently, in the wake of the pandemic, a group of researchers from several European countries looked at low-income families with preteen and teen children in the aftermath of the 2008 financial crisis in the United Kingdom, Portugal, and Norway. Based on their data, they concluded 'that publicly funded, nutritious school meals protect children from the direct effects of poverty on their food security, whilst underfunded and weakly regulated school food provision compounds children's experiences of disadvantage and exclusion'.[15]

We might believe that governments need to think about this more systematically, and we definitely should encourage them to do so, but in many parts of the world people are not waiting. Food banks or food hubs have sprung up, as ordinary citizens volunteer to provide access to surplus food for those in need, including school kids. From the more organised hubs, which use donations to fund their work, collecting surplus food from supermarkets and wholesalers and redistributing it to local charities, to the very local sites in a community centre or community garden, where people keep a refrigerator with eggs and fresh vegetables and encourage locals to take what they need. Governmental policy is slow and incremental; it will always be full of delays and reversals. And judging from the school meals often provided, both the nutritional value and taste are less than consistent with raising a healthy, satisfied population. Food banks and local centres are embedded in the communities in which they work and often have a greater sense of accountability than do governments—they are not going to push frozen pizza and jacket potatoes (usual staples on school menus) but are instead going to try to share fresh, locally grown produce, and to do so in a way that reduces overall waste. Local food for local people.

Take Oxford, in the United Kingdom, the home of dreaming spires and a world-class university, where 29 per cent of children live below the poverty line. Oxfordshire has eighty-three areas, and ten of them are among the 20 per cent most deprived in England. So groups like Oxford Food Hub, run exclusively by volunteers, work to help alleviate the food strain without waiting for the government to do something about it.[16] Supplying more than 150 organisations throughout Oxfordshire, OFH provides the equivalent of about twenty thousand meals a week—and that includes Oxford's schools.

So this first chapter on solutions is actually about leadership. Not about how to get it or improve it, but how to move away from it, and why we don't really seem to need it for some of the most important and immediate tasks facing us daily. This does not mean that we abolish government structures and rule as a mob. This does not mean that we disobey all laws and ignore the leaders that are already in place. It does not mean that we break existing rules and engage in disruptive behaviour to change policy. Rather, this means that we are actually going to move laterally by taking steps to begin building up the kind of inclusive self-care communities we want and need, as these examples have shown. When we, as properly self-organised citizens, know what we want and what we need, we can then move towards good, constructive versions of self-governance, in the form of actions we take as a group, decisions we make for our communities, and help we give one another. The process will leave less work for the elected leaders to do or will direct the elected representatives more effectively so that they are following *our* lead.

Critics might counter such claims by suggesting that the way forward entails just getting the right rules and maybe involving the public more directly in government processes and law making, like those in favour of lottocracy or sortition, democratic experiments in which citizens are randomly chosen to represent us all and make decisions that will hold for the polity. Some in this camp also believe that we can begin at the local level with these projects, scaling up to provide an alternative form of government at a national level.[17] I can see the draw and do think that dialogue and communication with local government is a first important step forward. But the thought of lottocracy in practice brings up very poor memories of jury duty on a cold Boston day, where we all sat convened in the room waiting for nothing, because the mere fact that we were assembled and ready to go to trial, with a judge on standby, meant that the parties involved were likely to bargain and accept an agreement in order to avoid the courtroom scene and an unpredictable outcome. I made not one friend during those long hours waiting, no one spoke to anybody else, no one was interested in anything but getting out of there. And this is, I fear, one problem with sortition as a solution to our current complaints. When people do not choose to come together but are brought together artificially for a cause or issue they may care nothing about, we cannot expect much in terms of solidarity.

Lottocracy and other forms of government by random citizen committee puts the cart before the horse, for suggesting such projects without first building up citizens as active, engaged representatives of the community is repeating the kind of problematic development that we have already gone through. We have seen examples of lottocracy and citizens' committees—both in the United Kingdom and France—where frustrated governments introduced these committees to debate and help propose legislation on complex issues like climate change and, more recently in France, euthanasia. In several cases, the experiments were highly criticised as mere sounding boards for government action, not true citizens' committees with legislative power or even influence. When I asked a French public intellectual recently for his opinion on these committees, he described them as 'bullshit', at least in the form they had taken to date in a democratic republic he has spent his career defending.

The philosopher Cristina Lafont points out that many of the alternative forms of representative democracy that have been suggested, such as lottocracy, still demand what she calls blind deference—deference of those being governed to the governors, no matter how selected or what number.[18] So the mini-publics that scholars advocate still swim in issues and criticisms. For me, they are problematic for these reasons but also because they focus on fixing the input mechanism for decisions, rather than thinking about democracy primarily in terms of actions.

Such proposals also demand a quality of strong social connection that you will not find in a large-scale area, whether a deliberative democracy or not. Take a step back for a minute and think about cardiovascular health. An important study looked at the likelihood of surviving for twelve months following a first heart attack. Among other things, the researchers found chances of survival were 50 per cent greater for people with 'strong social relationships'.[19] That placed strong and positive social relationships on par with quitting smoking and even more important than losing weight.

Taking such findings as a point of departure, evolutionary psychologists like Robin Dunbar investigated how adept we are at establishing strong social bonds, focusing on the neurological substrate of our brains and the most important cognitive mechanism that enables us to work within a stable group of stable relationships—a kind of social order. And the average size of the social network is only 150. This is Dunbar's number, and it traces across hunter-gatherers and armies and organisations and everyone in between; even the average size of English villages in the past was 150. And then he sees this reappear in the 250 species of primates. No primate has a group size of more than 50. But looking deeper, within this 150, the data shows that we are only really interacting in a strong and relatively stable friendship group of 4 or 5, even on Twitter or Facebook. The layers of social contact that he identified show emotional closeness among the innermost circle, the group most associated with physical and mental wellbeing. He also showed that we are happy to do a favour for someone within our broad group of 150 but not beyond, unless we also extract some benefit.[20] It is the group of 5, I propose, and the next concentric circles, that should be the basis for our citizenship groups. And the fact that we actually know one another and repeatedly interact to make relevant plans for our societies is key. It is the antithesis, in a way, of randomly chosen committees. Whether we agree or disagree with Dunbar's interpretation of the data and the subsequent popularisations, adaptations, and replications of this precise number, the point is that size matters. And smaller is best.

Scaling up, past that core social network, we risk moving away from exactly the kind of face-to-face local organisation that matters here, that makes democracy really work as true self-governance. And instead of abolishing the middleman immediately, choosing those who represent us from among those we already know creates a reciprocal relationship as a first step towards our ideal democracy—not a blind allegiance to what are in effect strangers, whom we allow to govern us while we get on with our jobs, our holidays, and our Netflix subscriptions.

A few decades ago I sat in a classroom that was already sweltering at nine in the morning and looked at a slide flash on a large screen. The image displayed was a foam structure that resembled a honeycomb. I was at the Santa Fe Institute in New Mexico, a place, you might say, committed to the butterfly effect—a term that derives from chaos theory, that branch of mathematics that has tried to understand and find patterns in the apparent randomness of the world's complex systems.[21] The young lecturer from Penn State University was perspiring as he described the process through which foam bubbles form a stable structure over time, a process known in fluid dynamics as coarsening. The best and most delicious example of the coarsening of a foam structure is a pint of Guinness, pulled from the tap. At first, the entire pint seems filled with beige cream. This cream is in fact not a single entity but a foam, millions of tiny bubbles stuck together, sharing sides which will, as the glass stands, change. Some bubbles will relax their sides and lose their gas to neighbouring bubbles. Then more will. And more, until most of the glass is made up of a mahogany-coloured beverage with a single layer of beige bubbles on top, in which most of the bubbles resemble one another roughly in size and shape. No one has done this for them. The bubbles have organised themselves. Provoked by the liquid's release from a tap, they have found the order that is right for them in that pint glass.

This process, the coarsening of a foam structure, the pulling of a pint of Guinness, happens on its own but so elegantly that it can be described by a mathematical formula.[22] And I believe the bubbles in Guinness teach us something very important about us: when left to their own devices, nature, the bubbles, find their way. Spontaneously, they arrange themselves in a structure that works well for all of them. For a while, they are in harmonious equilibrium, one that is noticeable: we can see it and taste it. No one tells them how to behave; they have self-organised, and, after enjoying that state of nirvana for a while, they will know when it is time to dissolve.

But when something disrupts their decentralised, natural process, we get either a flat mess or a different kind of order, a problematic one. In fluid dynamics this arrested development, which often sees one large bubble dominate, is known as the propagation of a single defect, and it is usually the result of human interference with the bubbles' natural process.

Let's imagine it: a disruption to the development of the bubbles as they are trying to self-organise in a lab dish. A single large bubble shows up in the dish through the lab technician's error, as he accidentally lets a bit of air come into the dish at the wrong time. This single air bubble is surrounded by smaller bubbles, trying to do their work but failing. As time passes, the central bubble gets larger, slowly dominating the space, like an autocrat. It takes air from neighbouring bubbles. Their sides collapse, and it becomes larger. I have seen this happen at the Santa Fe Institute. But I have also seen this happen in society—not with bubbles but people—throughout history.

Let's imagine that this large single bubble is the German Nazi Party, the Nationalsozialistische Deutsche Arbeiterpartei, which worked in a very organised and hierarchical way, via leadership that mobilised its members through a sociopathic mix of ruthlessness and charisma, taking 'air' and votes from the other political parties in Germany at that time, forcing some of them to collapse.[23] Eventually, the Nazi Party dominated the entire political space. You can see this, the fall of Weimar democracy and the subsequent rise of the Nazis, in a petri dish. Here in the lab is the closest, I think, to being there, seeing this collapse and the emergence of the Third Reich in person.

Of course, this is both an overly simplified and controversial way to think about the complexity of that period of world history. I should know, because I have written about it elsewhere, drawing from much more than a plastic lab dish: archives, interviews, and reputable scholars' research.[24] But it is an important analogy, because there are great similarities between the bubbles and us. For when a very stable order does emerge in societies, like in Nazi Germany, or in apartheid South Africa, it is often through a slow and gradual process of manipulation, and propaganda, and hierarchical control, displacing more decentralised and democratic processes. This stable, stifling order that emerges then works in tandem, codependently, with an oppressive leadership and often with laws as well—including constitutions—that allow such leadership to emerge.[25] Self-organisation is interrupted. With disastrous effect. We have always been told that nature needs authority for good order to exist. But nature does not, and in fact, nature risks suffocating under authority.

Back in Santa Fe that year, we decided to try again to grow a society of bubbles in a dish, this time using helium from a local party store to help speed up the process. After much discussion with party store staff about why we weren't interested in the free balloons, we left and went to work. When I arrived at the lab early the next day to examine the experiment, I did not find the solid structure I expected to see. No ordered honeycomb, but no single defect, either. *Nothing* had apparently happened. And then I noticed it, just before I turned and left the room— a crack in the Plexiglass frame on the left side, a crack which let air seep in, disturbing the entire set of bubbles as they were trying to make their good order. Some bubbles relaxed sides and joined forces with others, some disappeared. It seemed, very sadly, a failed experiment and a really big mess.

But as I looked more closely a smile came to my face.

'Le Pen!' I shouted. The young lecturer running the lab burst into laughter. His doctoral student in applied mathematics, apparently fed up with my bizarre analogies, rolled his eyes. He had a point. But here's the thing: when the extremist conservative leader Jean-Marie Le Pen first emerged in France in the 1970s, through the elections to the European Parliament, his group was small, even tiny. He was ostracised and kept at bay. He didn't seem to have a chance. He came from the sidelines, like a tiny bit of bad air seeping into the frame of a stable and democratic political structure.

Over time, something quite tremendous happened. His air, his message, started to spread. As people began voting for his party, he, this little bit of bad air, disrupted the equilibrium of the entire French political system. The conservative parties on the right lost air to him, the far-left parties lost air to him. The people on the extreme left and extreme right became sympathetic to his anti-immigrant rhetoric, his heralding of traditional 'French values'. And so all parties in the French political landscape changed shape as they moved around to make space for this bit of new air. So much so that, in 2002, Jean-Marie Le Pen, the racist, populist, and anti-democratic politician, made it to the second round of the French presidential elections. He became a player and a major one at that. Born into a frame by mistake, leaking through a tiny crack known as the European Parliament. Not unlike Donald Trump and other outsiders that we have seen emerge, quite gradually and surprisingly, in democracies. And all this, arguably, because once they broke through the crack in the frame and interrupted the natural settling of the other parties, our sets of electoral and constitutional rules then kicked in and made us vulnerable to playing follow the leader, even with a problematic one.

So don't play follow the leader. Act like a bubble instead. An empathetic, cooperative one at that.

CHAPTER THREE

Own Your Rights,
but Responsibly

I N 2005, I SAT IN THE BACK SEAT OF A RUSTY, SILVER
Renault, next to Hakim, the grand qadi of Mayotte,
whom we met earlier in this book. He was dressed in a
traditional white dishdasha, his hair wrapped and tucked
away into a mosaic turban. His broken glasses, held
together with sticky tape, slipped down his dark nose as
he slumped slightly to the right in the grey vinyl seat. We
were driving along National Route No. 1, destination

Mtsamboro, a small fishing village in the north of the main island, where there had been an unresolvable conflict. We were on our way to intervene.

We all shared an orange as the grand qadi explained the case. A young woman claimed she was being cheated out of her right to the family house. Hakim reminded me that in the seventh century, settlers from the Red Sea landed on these tiny islands off the coast of Madagascar to find a thriving Bantu African population ruled by a matriarchy. Women were strong and considered important. The settlers introduced Islam, setting up Islamic courts and a system of qadis, the Islamic judges. Islamic rules and laws coexisted with Bantu traditions and social norms, the latter being more salient for their daily lives. When the sultan of Mayotte then sold the islands to the French in the 1800s, Mayotte became part of the French Republic and, as such, fell under the French constitution. Superficially. Because these people were not exclusively French, or Muslim, or African. They were all these, and they were now governed by multiple rules, laws, and a constitution that was imposed by France directly on top of other cultural norms and traditions. Legal pluralism, as the anthropologists like to call it, now reigned.

It sounds unique and exotic. But once again, it is like most places in the world, including the United Kingdom and the United States, where multiple sets of rules coexist with traditions and layers of rule making and rule changing and govern peoples whose ancestry and identity are mixed and layered. And this is where things can go very wrong, when relying on the law to be the only way to adjudicate the distribution of rights can give us more problems than it solves.

Under the Bantu African matriarchal tradition, female children are respected and valued; they are well integrated, socially and financially. In their families, the mother plays a major, organising role.[1] So in Mayotte, which was certainly influenced by matriarchal traditions, custom dictated that when parents die, a girl inherits the family house first, before her brother has a right to it. If there is no house, her brother is obliged by custom to build one for her. This norm had existed and was appreciated as an element of social peace for centuries, even throughout the decades following the introduction of Islam.

When the French then introduced their secular law to the islands a century later, men on Mayotte had yet another set of rules to think about, including equality before the law. And according to French inheritance law, a brother now had a right to the same as his sister.

So how did this affect behaviour? Young people began to use laws strategically against one another, disrupting what had been a decent social fabric. According to Bantu tradition, male heirs would not have a right to the house if there was a female survivor who wanted it. According to French Republican law and the principle of equality, they should get equal shares. Did this French constitutional and legal principle lead to equality in Mayotte's inheritance law? No. Because the introduction of French law reminded men that according to the Islamic law which also existed at one time on their islands, men had a right to twice as much as women in inheritance. So, some of them began invoking Islamic law in inheritance cases which they had not done before, to gain more than an equal amount in some cases and, in a perversion of all law, as Hakim explained to me, to gain as much as they possibly could.

The introduction of codified written rules interrupted the social tradition and produced instead a melting pot of rules that led not only to confusion but also to strategically and selfishly picking and choosing the rules and laws that best suited individuals. It was worse than a mess: it was a gourmet tasting menu of some of the finest legal traditions—Islamic, French republican, Bantu—rather than a good social order, where rules facilitated a process of social disintegration.

Arguably, this outcome was inevitable, and it brought into relief the purpose of rules from the perspective of any self-preserving agent: gain. So, who cares?

We should. We must understand that Mayotte is not an exotic exception. Laws and rules and constitutions are often cloaks, thrown on and worn for performances, altered to suit political circumstances at any given time. Without these rules and laws, but with the knowledge of our rights, would we have more incentive to compromise and negotiate, to go back to social pacts and agreements based on community, trust, and shared identity? And wouldn't it be a more durable solution than simply clarifying and streamlining the laws (if that were even possible) and blaming legal pluralism for the problems? Because zero-sum, selfish gain is not part of being a good citizen. Instead, what we want to do if we are going to build a new type of citizen is understand that by restricting our own rights a little, we can help someone else enjoy their rights, too.

This entails owning our rights in a way that enables us to make agreements on when they can be exercised but also when we must choose to limit the expression of our right so that someone else's right will be protected. A bottom-up rights negotiation, not unlike the original Bantu solution to inheritance law. Practically, it means working towards mutual exchange and finding a basis for it, so that, for example, a gay couple can buy a cake for their wedding, even from a Christian baker, who is able to see the humanity of the couple in front of him rather than sexual preferences that conflict with his.

A sceptic may say, *Knowing what our rights are and how to protect them is hard for the average Joe, so why not let the law, the constitution, do the work for us? The law tells us whether we can legally have intercourse in the privacy of our own homes. Whether we can marry and enjoy the financial protection of the state. It tells us whether we can legally own weapons. Whether we can help someone in deep pain end their life. Whether a woman can legally have an abortion in her local town. It tells us all these difficult things, doesn't it? Let's let the court and the judges decide and the police enforce.*

Well, the constitution and the laws and the justices do not tell us these things clearly. Most often, they tell us ambiguously, just as the US Supreme Court did in *Roe v Wade* and then in *Dobbs v Jackson*. And this is the problem with leaving all rights decisions completely and exclusively to the law.

Consider some of the ambiguity: if it were so clear cut, would nine highly educated and informed scholars of law disagree about what the 'right' thing to do really is? Would they disagree as much as the justices of the US Supreme Court have done for decades and continue to do?

Constitutional interpretation—trying to understand what our rights are and whether or not we are actually enjoying them—is our task, the task we all have as bearers of rights. But we have long lost our ability to interpret. Our own muscles for interpreting have become weak. Quite some time ago, shortly after our constitutions were made, we gradually handed over the task of not only writing the constitution but also interpreting it—of trying to understand, for example, whether a sex act was protected by our right to privacy—to judges who acted as custodians of our rights. This was not the original idea of the Supreme Court in the United States but one that evolved when ordinary legislation came into conflict with the Constitution. As our constitutions grew in length and complexity, and our body of ordinary law also grew, with more rights and more obligations and more limitations, we needed someone else to keep track of the conflicts between them. And this is the gradual drift that resulted in less thinking on our part, because we entrusted someone else to decide these things for us.

But constitutional interpretation, when done by judges, is a form of translation. Someone must translate the written word that was recorded long ago. In the United States, for example, they were other Americans, living 250 years ago in a very different America. Now we must translate that constitutional document not into a different language but into a different era and for different peoples. Our circumstances, our contexts, our races, our technology, our ideas of gender and equality, and many of our core values have changed, sometimes dramatically so. Can the translation, the interpretation, really be done, justly, fairly, for all? Can the written word in the text be translated to provide justice for real people who have real conflicts in real time? And what of countries with strict secular constitutions, such as France with its particular form known as *laïcité* and Germany, whose recent immigrants, practising Muslims from former colonies, find no space for religious expression in the public sphere because even their dress is sometimes outlawed according to the interpretation of constitutional texts?

Traduttore, traditore. Translator, traitor. So charged the Italians in the sixteenth century, as numerous French translations of their beloved Dante proliferated. To translate, they charged, is to betray. And there is only one thing that can be done to prevent it. We must stop translating.

We must learn the language of our rights instead. We must do it ourselves.

Here is one example, and a tragic one. In the 1980s, four-year-old Joshua DeShaney was so severely beaten by his father that he fell into a coma. Emergency brain surgery revealed haemorrhages caused by traumatic injuries suffered over a long period of time. Joshua's mother sued the Winnebago County Department of Social Services for violation of Joshua's liberty and equality before the law, according to the Fourteenth Amendment of the US Constitution, demonstrating that the DSS was aware of the repeated abuse and did nothing to intervene. When Joshua's case came before the US Supreme Court, a majority ruled that, constitutionally, the DSS was not responsible for protecting Joshua in this way and so did not fail in its responsibility to the boy.

'Poor Joshua! . . . It is a sad commentary upon American life, and constitutional principles—so full of late of patriotic fervor and proud proclamations about "liberty and justice for all"—that this child, Joshua DeShaney, now is assigned to live out the remainder of his life profoundly retarded.' So wrote Justice Harry Blackmun, dissenting from the majority opinion of his court and its interpretation of the Constitution. Essentially proving that Leviathan was divided and confused, Justice Blackmun said it plainly: the Constitution does not give us order and justice. And authority can do little about it because that authority itself is divided.

Elena Kagan, a current US Supreme Court justice, was a young law clerk there when Joshua's case came before the court for consideration. Kagan wrote a memo urging them not to take the case *because it was so important*.[2] Her reasoning? There were positive signs that at lower-level courts or districts, in a decentralised way, judges and individuals in local government were beginning to read positive obligations into the Constitution: positive obligations that would protect more Joshuas from harm, that would encourage more responsibility on the part of local social services that were negotiating rights from the bottom up. Given the political makeup of the court at that time, with a conservative majority, Kagan feared a negative decision, one that would be a binding precedent throughout the United States and stop the spontaneous, positive rights negotiation that was already occurring without the supreme authority of the court. Her fear became reality.

And, perhaps most important of all, the issues not before the court that day: Where were the neighbours in this case? The community? Where were the good Samaritans? Why did we all do nothing and then sympathise with the dissenting opinion of the US Supreme Court to make us feel the pain of poor Joshua's fate and then acquiesce in the Supreme Court's ruling?

What we need to understand is that laws and constitutions are not the ultimate answer to a good life, and they can actually harm us in important ways, by failing us, by opening themselves to interpretations that do not protect us, and by then setting them in stone—or at least making them very difficult to change. They can also, as in the religious freedom cases, cause such conflict and disorder that individuals are left to their own devices, scrambling for a way out like insects in a web. And perhaps most crucially, they fail us if they take our rights from us, only to give them back according to a set of rules introduced by a group of people from a time long, long ago in what might sometimes seem like a galaxy far away. Witness the recent decision of the US Supreme Court on abortion. In *Dobbs v Jackson*, a majority of the court decided that the majority of the court deciding *Roe v Wade*, the previous landmark case on abortion, was wrong—that the US Constitution does *not* contain a right to abortion and that it is up to individual states to legislate this right.

'Legal interpretation takes place in a field of pain and death.' So begins a famous article by one of the most interesting legal scholars of our time, Robert Cover, a former Yale Law School professor. Indeed, and as Cover went on to claim, 'a judge articulates her understanding of a text, and as a result, somebody loses his freedom, his property, his children, even his life'.[3] This is what Cover called the 'violence of the word'. Writing in the mid-1980s, Cover was witnessing this interpretation all around him, and it seemed to scare the bejesus out of him. Because constitutions can actually harm us, by opening themselves to interpretations, which they must do. Interpretations do not always protect us, and yet a judge's interpretation can and will affect people, both in the quality of their lives and the quantity. A judge's interpretation can also cause such conflict and disorder that individuals are left scrambling for a way out of what should have been a solution. What good does that scramble do to promote social peace?

There is a popular hypothetical case that American law professors use in their courses every year. Written in 1949 by Lon Fuller, it imagines five cave explorers in the fifth millennium who become trapped and, through a series of decisions made under extreme stress, kill and eat one member of their group to survive.[4] Once rescued, they are put on trial for murder and, following the law of the time, sentenced to death. The supreme court deciding their fate has seven justices, each with a different interpretation of both the law and the facts of the case. Since its original publication over half a century ago, well-known legal scholars have created more hypothetical justices and more possible opinions. The point of the exercise: to introduce law students to the impossibility of interpretation and at the same time, the dramatic consequences of this necessary impossibility.

Consider a similar but this time real situation in which everyone disagrees, and a judge needs to interpret the Constitution quickly because an ill teenage boy's life is at stake. In 2007, a few days after Thanksgiving Day, a young American, Dennis Lindberg, was in this very situation. A Jehovah's Witness through his grandmother's influence and only fourteen years old, Dennis died of leukaemia just hours after the Skagit County Superior Court in the state of Washington upheld his right to refuse a blood transfusion that would have saved his life based on his constitutional right to religious freedom. The judge in this case stated that the boy was 'basically giving himself a death sentence' but supported his right to do so, noting that because of his religion, 'he believes with the transfusion he would be unclean and unworthy'.[5]

As an American living for the past decades in Europe, I often look back at the United States like an astronaut seeing the earth for the first time from outer space. There is often an incredible clarity to the view from here, for the particular American conception of liberty, as protected by our Constitution, allows for a variety of both private and public practices, from the right to free speech, even controversial 'hate speech', to exemptions from the law on the grounds of religious accommodation. It is a different world from Europe, influenced both by Roman law and the aftermath of war and communism, where the individual does not reign. In the case of Dennis Lindberg, the judge hearing the case had nothing against which Dennis's constitutional right to religious freedom could be balanced so that his life could be saved. No obligation to save his life was found in the Constitution. Not because it did not exist but because—and this is the key—it was not translated into the text. The judge did not 'find' it, did not interpret the text in a way that allowed him to uncover this obligation there. But maybe he could have. There was disagreement: from the doctors treating Dennis, who were bound by the code of ethics of the American Medical Association and wanted to save his life. From Dennis's parents, who wanted him to live and who were not religious. And finally, of course, from Dennis, who said he was bound by the laws of his religion, protected by the US Constitution. When these 'rules'—the Constitution and the medical code of ethics and the religious laws of the Jehovah's Witnesses—came into conflict, together with the various and differing opinions of Dennis's parents, doctors, grandmother, and Dennis himself, where was the good order, the justice, to be found? Dennis, a fourteen-year-old boy in a precarious mental and physical state, died. Weren't rules, laws, and, above all, constitutions supposed to protect him, the most vulnerable among us, the sick and underaged? Dennis did not want to die, but he did not want to live with what his religion told him was dirty blood. So he decided in favour of death, his only option. This is justice?

Compare this to the case of another young person. In the 1980s, the fate of young Karen Ann Quinlan gripped a nation. A hitherto unknown twenty-one-year-old from Pennsylvania, Quinlan became one of the most debated figures in the United States for nearly a decade. Having suffered a coma after consuming Valium and alcohol, Quinlan fell into a persistent vegetative state. Her parents, practising Catholics, requested she be taken off her respirator, believing that it caused her pain. Doctors refused, though there was evidence that she was effectively brain-dead. Her parents sought an authority to untie the Gordian knot: in 1975, they filed a lawsuit which made its way on appeal to the New Jersey Supreme Court. In 1976, the court found in Quinlan's right to privacy a justification for her parents' request, and her respirator was disconnect-ed.[6] Quinlan continued to live and was fed by artificial nutrition for nine more years until she suffered respiratory failure and died naturally in 1985.

A judge might have just as easily *not* found in Quinlan's right to privacy a right not to be on a respirator. Finding rights, but also not finding rights, is the ongoing business of judicial interpretation. But what is to say that the rights that are found, or are not found, are correct, that the process provides justice for all? The Constitution of the United States of America coexists, like all other constitutions around the world, with numerous other laws, rules, and codes but also next to long-standing traditions and beliefs. Just as in our story of Mayotte. In the United States' sister republic, France, judges have often denied religious citizens—and this includes adults—the religious right to refuse medical treatment, citing an obligation to preserve life above all else. Similar constitutions, similar rights, similar challenges. Very different interpretations. Very different translations.

Some of these examples may seem anomalies in an oth-erwise just system, obscure, media-worthy tearjerkers. But they are not. They are examples of what happens in our democracies every single day: somewhere, a judge is inter-preting our constitution, and, in so doing, they are making a life-or-death decision. Who is to say that their decision is the 'right' one, the right interpretation? And are those who disagree wrong? Often they are not. Constitutional interpretation, and legal interpretation more generally, is a matter of opinion, and, as such, someone else's opinion is necessarily betrayed. Much is, to quote a cliché, lost in translation.

To take yet another example, in October 2004, a fifteen-year-old Muslim girl from Strasbourg demonstrated the problem poignantly: she shaved her head in order to be able to attend school, claiming that this act was the only way for her to simultaneously respect both the new French law on secularism governing her public life that prohibited Islamic headscarves in state schools and the long-standing Islamic law governing her conscience that required her to cover her hair in public. A bald head allowed her to get around the rule problem. It was a spontaneous way to find an equilibrium that allowed this young woman to go to school. The rules, laws, and constitution of France did not necessarily protect her and aid her in this complex situation, though they claimed to.[7] They caused disorder, and she found a way out. But perhaps not the way she would have chosen, had there been alternatives.

These are a few individual cases, but there are many like them. They all point to a fact that is everywhere, every day, and is undeniable: some very well-designed rules and rule sets, such as laws and especially constitutions, do fail to protect our rights. They fail to safeguard us from harm. Sometimes, as in the cases above, their articles and amendments allow for dangerous practices and absolve the state from responsibility to help us, although we are in many ways relying on it to do so.

Supreme courts like that found in the United States do this. They are the highest level of court in the judicial system, so the highest appellate court, but they are also protectors of constitutions. Constitutional courts are a different type of beast, but they do this, too.[8] They also exist to guard the constitution, but they exist outside of the regular structure of the judicial branch of government, and constitutional protection is their main task. What's more, in some countries, these constitutional courts can even engage in abstract review—whereby judges can offer opinions that are not yet based on any concrete case of conflict before the court. In others, such as Germany, constitutional courts can be accessed directly by individual citizens, through an individual petition, if a person can show that they have exhausted all other forms of redress and that their rights have been violated.

Both supreme courts and constitutional courts are there to make sure the Leviathan, whom we trusted with our order, is still doing it according to the main rules, the higher law, and our agreed values. This can and has been useful. But we are increasingly diverse societies, and often even when we agree on the main values and an accepted hierarchy of them, we cannot always agree on the interpretation of these values or their limits. I am not suggesting that we should do away with bills of rights in constitutions, or even constitutions themselves. Eventually, perhaps, but that is a long way off. And certain rights, such as medical rights that affect life and death, do need some rudder, some form of regulation, while we figure out what to do. So for now, they must exist—but we should work towards a future in which they at least do not take centre stage. Rather, constitutions should be the minimal frameworks within which we work, the understudies in our dramas. We must seek our own fluid orders, agree on our own justice. We must show civil obedience, but to ourselves and all within our communities. We must own our rights, but responsibly so.

We will need to limit the full exercise of our own rights sometimes to protect the rights of someone else. This is a negotiation, one that we will need to engage in every single day.[9] And it is a negotiation that will sometimes fail, because some individuals will refuse to give up what they consider their due share. The possibilities for and promise of increasing this negotiation, widening that space for it, come down to our agreed understanding of justice. Make no mistake, it is not the vigilante justice of Clint Eastwood or Quentin Tarantino I am calling for, however satisfying some of the endings of their films might at first seem. Nor is it an endorsement of organised crime, that hierarchical form of state defection, even if we do recognise that organised criminal groups also question existing laws and authority structures and, in so doing, present an alternative state-making project.[10] But it *is* perhaps a reaction I have had to the world described by Al Pacino in his closing statement as the rebel attorney for the defence in a 1970s courtroom drama: 'Justice for all. Only we have a problem here. Both sides want to win. We want to win regardless of the truth. And we want to win regardless of justice.'[11]

Because justice, as I now discuss with my students in Bologna, is not an inherent quality written into a document. It is not an objective thing. Justice is a subjective perception of fairness, and as such it can truly exist only as an internal virtue. As we all know, what seems right and fair is hardly universally agreed upon. There will be controversy. There will be winners and losers. But we cannot just leave it to the constitution or the courts. Here there is, among everyone else, competition and ego, financial incentives and constraints. In taking over so much of our work and gaining so much importance in our lives, by delegating to a judge the burden of deciding what is fair and what is not, we have lost our appreciation of what justice really is and have allowed a hollow sense of it to reign. Instead, we need to understand how we can do some of this, how we can start a bottom-up rights negotiation. How, for example, people in a small town can together decide whether a park statue violates the rights of a particular group and then collectively remove it from view or cover it up or turn it around, and can agree that the importance of the call to prayer to even just some of their neighbours means that it should not constitute a noise offence. Little examples with big messages that together help us understand our fellow citizen. Collectively deciding what, as Michael Sandel puts it with simple elegance, is the 'right thing to do'.[12]

Almost two decades ago, a group of neighbours decided to take Oxford City Council to court to protect nine acres of undeveloped land in North Oxford once owned by St John's College. It was 'scrubland', with reed beds and on what the presiding judge Lord Hoffmann described as 'not idyllic' property now owned by the City of Oxford; only 25 per cent was accessible, and then only to the 'hardy walker'. The question was, who had a right to this land? The city council owned it and hoped to sell it to a developer for social housing in the already built-up and expensive urban area. Bulldozers were about to move in, but this group of locals, in an act that some have even interpreted as a NIMBY problem, successfully prevented it by using a legal device: cleverly having it established as a 'village green'. Hardy walking is not the first phrase that comes to mind with a village green, and for this legal device to work, the concept, the meaning, of village green needed to be reinterpreted to include this space. If it was indeed to be understood as an area for leisure pursuits and pastimes, then the plaintiffs in this case would need to demonstrate that it was one. In a landmark decision of the High Court, the concept of the village green was interpreted to incorporate this space.[13]

And yet, only a decade later, those who had opened up the space by invoking this very clever legal idea also made it effectively into a nature reserve and determined their own rules for the space.[14] Signs posted ask for 'no jogging or cycling', and there is only one obvious entrance. When asked by some local residents to open the green more, to include more locals, and to improve access and use, some members of the original group claimed it would harm the local wildlife. Though it is a lovely if still hardy space now, rich with fauna and flora, thanks to the hard work of the locals who take care of the trees and remove debris, and meant to be enjoyed by all, the interpretation of what that means is apparently determined by only a few.[15]

Why do the rights of one group of citizens effectively trump the rights of the others? The lives of others? The lives of the poor and homeless? We have sometimes forgotten what the rights of others are, and we have forgotten how to move across our group to understand and respect the rights of the other: across racial and ethnic, religious and gender, socioeconomic lines, but also across the lines marked by age, to include as many citizens as possible. As the urban planner Yasminah Beebeejaun says, 'The realization of legal rights or protections is not experienced innately as if there were a direct correlation between legislation and everyday life. Rather, everyday life is a complex negotiation where the concepts and practices of citizenship, exclusions, and prejudice are experienced and co-constituted with other urban dwellers. Our rights are embodied and form the sites where assumptions are made about our subject positions.'[16] It's an academic statement, made for an academic audience. But her meaning here is both simple and profound: rights are really negotiated democratically when we bump up against one another in these spaces, where our interactions with one another then shape who we are, and how we use and take ownership of our rights so that others can, too.

This, I believe, is justice. And this is also true citizenship, for it does not exclusively involve and depend upon the state's extension and protection of our rights and our passive acquiescence in whatever the state provides. Instead of being the subjects of the state, I suggest that we be the agents. Obviously, there are limits. We are not vigilantes. We cannot make our own decisions about life and death in the absence of some guiding structure and expert medical knowledge. We should not, I believe, arm ourselves, whatever the constitution may tell us is our legal right to do, nor should we use violent means to accomplish our goals. Obviously, some of the most difficult decisions—the right to abortion, the right to have help ending one's life—will always be surrounded by divisive, polarised debate. We know this. So the current challenge is finding a way to work through and negotiate the issues that are not life or death first, those that are workable and even easy in comparison, until we are ready to move on to higher stakes.

Imagine as an example a community that offers uneducated or economically underprivileged women and girls, but also men and boys, unbiased, medically vetted information about contraception and family planning; that helps cross racial and religious boundaries while discussing these things practically and meaningfully, so that fewer unwanted pregnancies occur. So, when pregnancies do result from rape or incest, or medical complications leave foetuses or their mothers with complex medical conditions, perhaps courts will then not hesitate to offer a legal and medically sound and unproblematic way to end the pregnancy without the prejudice or harassment that these women sometimes currently face.[17]

Our rights are at the forefront of many debates now—from gay marriage to religious expression, to freedom of speech; from abortion and the right to life, freedom of movement, the right to refuse vaccinations, digital privacy, and so forth. Discussing and showing how these rights can be protected by our own negotiation (rather than leaving it to the law) is at the core of this model of citizenship. So if the courts are not the answer, what or who is, and how will it actually work?

In legal philosophy and constitutional theory, the discussion has been robust, as scholars have contended with how we might have more control over the decisions that structure our everyday lives, from budgets and national spending to official languages and holidays. But they have also increasingly wondered how we might gain more control over tough, divisive issues about our fundamental rights. Mark Tushnet was one of these scholars. His career began as a clerk at the US Supreme Court in the 1970s, where he helped draft one of the memos that was critical for the court's decision on abortion in *Roe v Wade*. Through the decades that followed, Tushnet became one of the most cited scholars of constitutional law, eventually arguing for, and I quote the title of one of his books, 'taking the constitution away from the court'. In this book, Tushnet detailed a project he called 'populist constitutional law', which he believed should be the way we protect our universal human rights, justified through reason, and allowing for reason-giving debate among the various peoples involved. Tushnet wanted to take some of the most divisive decisions of our time away from the courts and hand them back to democratically elected bodies such as legislatures. This would not necessarily mean better decisions, Tushnet cautioned, but it would mean that these decisions were, procedurally, in terms of how they were made, closer to the people affected by them. That is, these decisions would be overtly political: deliberated and discussed by politicians who, unlike most judges on high courts, can be voted out through regular elections. Better decisions would not necessarily follow, but the mechanism for how these decisions were reached (public discussion and voting) and the stability of these decisions (possible fluctuations with electoral cycles) would differ fundamentally from the elite model of constitutionalism in which unelected scholars of the law made decisions that would be pretty much carved in stone across jurisdictions. Popular constitutionalism, and other versions which scholars are now referring to as deliberative constitutionalism, are hot topics in legal theory these days. Persuaded, finally, by the crumbling political structures of representative government, with the emergence of not only poor leaders but also poor decisions and in some cases poorly protected rights, many academics in political philosophy and law are asking whether there are different ways to do constitutionalism.

For decades I was also persuaded by Tushnet's work, believing that the heavy lifting still needed to be done through formal institutions of some kind, just more deliberative and inclusive ones. But after some time, a lot of experience abroad, and one stint as co-secretary of my daughter's school PTA, I came to understand that for such a model to work, for popular constitutionalism or deliberative constitutionalism to mean something real, a first step was blatantly missing: the real power in all of this lies with citizens themselves, not through formal structures but informal, fluid ones. And by tackling the not-so-big questions first. We the citizens, we the peoples, can and should do constitutionalism, not through referenda or plebiscites (mechanisms that leave little room for negotiation in that they are zero-sum, discrete moments of decision making), but also not through jury systems or mini-publics which amount to committees decided by lot (mechanisms that will still include voting, though perhaps at least with increased deliberation), but rather, through continuous groundwork, what I am going to call for the sake of emphasis 'guerrilla constitutionalism'. Crazy, I know. But here is what I mean.

To begin, we could do as much as possible to set up the best initial conditions for guerrilla constitutionalism. That means adequate education for all of the community, through literacy and information campaigns, so that the person on the street has the tools to understand and think through the issues, not just accept the elite spin about them. In a perfect world, we would ensure everyone has access to unbiased information and knows how to spot bias where it pops up. This will be hard. Surely those with the best broadband are getting faster connections, but that does not mean they are getting better information. And social media has inundated our lives, to the point of saturation, and often with algorithms that are clearly biased, encouraging hate speech, affecting electoral outcomes, and escalating problems we are trying to get away from.[18] We might increasingly see regulatory bodies entrusted by governments to review and monitor this information, but we cannot, should not, rely on them exclusively to do so. So we need much more thinking about ways to empower all individuals in a decentralised space, so that we can all look at information with a critical eye.

Practically, we will want our public spaces to be equipped with daily news reports for those who will not access them through cell phones. If the local newsstand selling papers and displaying their front pages in a town square was once the place for people to stop and, without even purchasing anything, glance at the headlines from various publications and chat with the news seller about the latest juicy bits, today's equivalent could see environmentally discreet, solar-powered plasma screens displaying information from a variety of sources, with optional soundscapes for the visually impaired. Such respectful installations have been a part of public outdoor museums for some years now, around the world, including Holocaust memorials in Germany. More recently, One Planet in Australia used urban screens to offer public information campaigns, and London-based Climavore, which calls itself a community interest company made up of a team of artists, uses installations to raise awareness and provoke debate about adaptive eating, asking us as a public to confront and reflect upon how climate change demands a different approach to human consumption. Climavore calls its work 'site responsive iterations'.[19] This is what we need more of, as a beginning. Site-responsive iterations. Not static but dynamic forms of varied information that invite us, encourage us to learn and engage, deliberate and debate information together before we accept it and decide what to do with it.[20]

Plenty of philosophers, including Benedict Anderson and G. W. F. Hegel, were struck by the daily printed newspaper as not only a source of information but almost as a substitute for morning prayers in a secular world. Reading the morning paper is an act, according to Anderson, 'performed in silent privacy, in the lair of the skull'. But—and this is the key we want to then use—Anderson said that each person reading the paper was aware that this little ceremony of his was being replicated by thousands or millions of others. 'What more vivid figure for the secular, historically clocked, imagined community can be envisioned?' he asked.[21] Anderson went on to describe that same reader observing replicas of his own paper being read on the train or in any public space, and therefore being reassured that this imagined community was in fact 'rooted in everyday life'. These days, we don't know, when we see people looking at their phones on the underground or at the park, what they are actually reading. The confidence in community—or at least in the observation that we are reading the same news, that we are bound by the same narratives—has arguably disappeared with the emergence of the internet and our cellular phones. We need to be back in the physical space, the piazzas, with publicly shared information—for without such markers we are everywhere 'connected' by social media and yet at the same time atomised.

From there, from this modest but critical starting point, we can begin to provide a basis for discussion on an open and even and informed playing field, which is the only kind of playing field that can be legitimate for thinking about and taking the kinds of tough decisions that we find enshrined in constitutional court documents: same-sex marriage, abortion, euthanasia, religious expression, and so on. Inevitably, it comes back to finding a way to help us own our rights again, and own them responsibly.

Such guerrilla constitutionalism can and will work only if the conditions are right for it, and shared information is only one of them. Albert Hirschman, the developmental economist, talked about the importance of backward and forward linkages.[22] Hirschman suggested that for a certain sector of the economy to develop, backward linkages (in the form of helpful inputs) needed for that sector to work would find an opportunity to exist, and forward linkages would then also develop as opportunities popped up to utilise and take advantage of the sector's outputs. For guerrilla constitutionalism to work, the backward and forward linkages must be there, for on its own a popular rights negotiation remains an embattled, flawed utopia. But imagine that we ensure that kids are given the proper starting point, that public physical spaces encourage the kind of free and accurate sharing of information that is critical to public debate, deliberation, and general engagement that opens communication and fosters common knowledge: here we have some backward linkages. Then, we see less of a focus on leadership; this new sector of citizens gets communities to concentrate on being self-sufficient and sustainable, and so these communities openly embrace the reality of mosaics that make us one community, thinking about and discussing rights, maybe moving towards some of the citizens' committees that make big decisions about incredibly important issues, such as euthanasia. Then we will have the necessary backward *and* forward linkages that will support our guerrilla constitutionalism.

Clearly, we also need to help people feel safe in their spaces, so that guerrilla constitutionalism can work. This is perhaps one of the most important prerequisites, or backward linkages, along with access to unbiased information. Fortunately, we have evidence that we can do this, if with some growing pains and leaps of faith. Recently in Brownsville, a neighbourhood of Brooklyn, New York, local police officers agreed to stand aside and let residents police themselves, even responding to 911 emergency calls. The five-day experiment led by the Brownsville In Violence Out (BIVO) organisation, supported by the local authorities, was for many a success. Now at several points during the year, police step aside for a five-day stretch, allowing the organisation to step in and mediate. Its members do not carry weapons; they do not use violent means. But so far these resident groups have 'persuaded people to turn in illegal guns, prevented shoplifting, kept a man from robbing a bodega and stopped a pregnant woman from hitting a boyfriend who had not bought a car seat and a stroller as he had promised'.[23] And this is just the beginning. As part of a public health Cure Violence model, this programme follows evidence-based examples of making communities, particularly troubled ones, safer places for citizens to interact. Among other things, BIVO uses what they call 'credible messengers'—residents who have grown up on the same streets and either been involved in or exposed to gun violence—to interrupt violence, mediate on the spot where violence is imminent, and spread more positive narratives and opportunities in the community. They are credible because they are local, and they have the 'been there, done that' attitude that allows them to be horizontally linked to the community, rather than standing above or outside of it.[24] Local, credible, spontaneous, and horizontal support for local people. This is an important element of guerrilla constitutionalism. For when groups like this begin to offer real alternatives to both state control of their communities and total, lawless anarchy—a safe area between them which helps people understand how they can exercise their rights while protecting the rights of others—the need and desire to hide behind and rely exclusively on the law dissolves.

These ideas—focusing on eradicating the disparities that allow large segments of our communities to remain uninformed and therefore disengaged—and others have always been seen as the prerequisites for democracy in the academic disciplines concerned with democratic theory.[25] How and why they have been lost over decades, letting legal scholars and political scientists focus almost exclusively on institutions and leaders, is baffling.[26] For in addressing the prerequisites of democracy instead, we might one day see that we rely less on institutions because we have the capacity, and the capabilities, for doing the heavy lifting ourselves. And this is where we will begin to really own our own rights—when we are able to be ultrasocial, as the psychologists and biologists say. Some of the most important work being done now across species and across continents brings together psychologists, economists, anthropologists, biologists, and mathematicians, among others, to study the conditions necessary for the kind of cooperation and trust that happens not just within a group that looks and acts and has the same values as we do but, most importantly, across these groups.

One very hot spring back in Oxford, the PTA of my daughter's school decided to resume their lolly sales on Fridays, after a long hiatus during the pandemic. These had been very popular and fun events for the community, opportunities to come together and share an after-school treat which signalled the beginning of summer to the kids and brought in a little money for the school. Our dilemma? What price to sell these lollies for. The school is a state primary with nearly half the children speaking English as an additional language and a not negligible number of children dependent on free school meals. We as the PTA wondered how we might price the lollies to increase the chances that all children who wanted one could afford it, while also at least covering our costs if not making some profit for the practical items, the balls and hula hoops, needed for the school. I reached out to data scientist Gary

King, who suggested what we can call the 'donation solution'. We made the lollies free but asked for donations from those who could afford it, making it clear that the amount was up to them and that any and all profits would go to buy materials for the school. The result was a resounding success, with quite a few people giving more than the original price idea of one pound. Many simply 'overpaid'. They didn't have to. But here's why they did.

First, experiments from economics and psychology tell us that framing can be really important. If we frame issues to encourage a cooperative, altruistic decision that allows people to own their rights responsibly, rather than in a selfish way, we are already on the right track.[27] So in our case, we explained that the donations don't go to an ice-cream seller or even to a good but distant cause but instead that all the profits from these donations benefit all the children in the school. Second, experiments also tell us that when people are asked to give money for an item that is clearly considered by them to be a luxury, such as a lolly, they are more willing to donate than if it were a necessity, and they are even often willing to overpay for this luxury. They, we, are more willing to want to share. This is what social scientists sometimes refer to as 'warm glow giving'.[28] According to this idea, we do indeed make a donation, or we help a stranger in some other way, but not out of a completely pure, altruistic motivation. Rather, the warm glow we get from helping is a personal benefit which we obviously value, and this motivates us to act.

Well, I'll settle for that for now. Because whichever conception of humanity we subscribe to, be it a self-interested individual or an altruistic one, the evidence shows that people can and will help one another under the right circumstances.[29] We will reduce or limit our right to something so that another can benefit, too. Framing the issue properly and tapping into warm glow giving are among the first steps in our guerrilla constitutionalism, steps that encourage us because they help us understand that, by restricting my rights a little, I can actually help someone else enjoy their rights as well. Wouldn't that be worth it?

Will there be freeloaders, individuals who take advantage of this generosity? Surely. But perhaps the risk is worth it, and perhaps there are some gentle ways to keep the freeloaders on board with the rest of us.

Warm glow giving for a bottom-up rights negotiation, as the foundation of our guerrilla constitutionalism, seems like a lot to ask. And sure, rights are a very different 'good'—we can make more money, but can we make more rights if we give up ours? Well, let's take the example of sexual orientation and cake. When supreme courts in the United States and the United Kingdom were debating whether it was constitutional for a Christian baker to refuse to make a cake for a gay wedding, or to write 'support gay marriage' on it with buttercream icing, I reached out to one such cake maker on the internet.[30] 'I would make a cake or a home-cooked meal for *anyone* who asked,' she replied. 'Just like God would impart His love on anyone who asked. There are no exceptions for me.'[31] Warm glow rights giving. Owning your rights, but responsibly. Negotiating them from the bottom up and in so doing, reimagining your rights and owning the process. Having some of your cake but making sure your neighbour can have some of theirs, too.

CHAPTER FOUR

Hang Out in a Piazza, Repeatedly

T HEY SAY IN THE AMERICAN SITCOM *CHEERS* THAT sometimes you just want to go where everybody knows your name. This sitcom message is actually true, because what research has shown us across time and space is that, yes, for the most part, we do tend to want to go where we are known and liked. Having a space where we can go regularly, where we feel known and accepted, is also important politically. The physical community, the tangible public sphere, our associational life, is absolutely critical to our democracy.[1] These spaces, these open free spaces, which I broadly refer to as the piazza, have little to do with the law as we know it. Because law as we know it and have developed it in the modern world stems not from cooperation in open spaces but from conflict and its resolution.

Remove yourself for the moment from the comforting space of the pub or bar or café, where you are enjoying a drink and speaking with people who know you and are willing to listen to you complain about politics, or your job, or your needy relatives. Instead imagine a patch of dirt in medieval England, where two nervous men are positioning themselves to settle their disagreement with swords. The crowd around them is transfixed by this scene, gasping with both fear and excitement, mesmerised by that force that grips our psyche and asks us to watch the thrill of the battle and to speculate about defeat. It is, without the physical violence, not unlike the televised trials that grip our attention. Remember any of them, from O. J. Simpson to Johnny Depp to Gwyneth Paltrow. Remember how some of us watched, almost against our better judgement, like heads out of car windows, gaping as we slowed down to pass by the scene of a horrific accident. We felt compelled to look. We felt relieved that we were not ourselves involved.

There is no coincidence between these two scenes, no forced analogy—even though many centuries may separate them. The duel by sword is the origin of the adversarial legal system we live by today in our so-called civilised countries.[2] Indeed, 'the power dynamics laid bare in battle and ordeal will be familiar to any American trial attorney today'.[3] We may have moved indoors, from the patch of dirt to the sterile and orderly theatre of the court-room. But the structure remains—the defence of honour, of right and wrong, of justice and its zero-sum nature are all still here. And whether on the dirt patch or in the clean courtroom, the point is that this form of resolving differences has little to do with cooperation, for the duel was often to the death and the outcome of the courtroom is almost never a win-win situation: it usually means that one person's gain is equal to the other person's loss. Now in practice one might say that if justice is achieved, if the message sent through society has positive effects on the behaviour of generations to come, then it is not a complete loss for one party; there are future gains for all. But as James Marshall, member of the New York State Bar and both litigator and scholar, once said:

> The popular concept of the law, reinforced by literature and T.V. shows, is that it is principally involved in litigation conducted by hard-hitting or cleverly devious adversaries before ignorant juries and a judge who may be a model of justice, a jackass, or corrupt. One side is right, the other is wrong. One side tries to establish truth, the other to obfuscate it. This view of the law is like the legendary ideal of war depicted in the face-to-face

battles of the mighty fighters of the *Iliad*. This popular view . . .
is nevertheless accurate insofar as the adversary system creates
what game-theorists speak of as a zero-sum situation.[4]

We need only to think about some of the recent high-
profile cases which seemed to work this way, such as *Roe
v Wade* in the United States in 1973, which protected an
individual's liberty to have an abortion. It was met not
only with genuine elation by some but also vehement dis-
approval by others. It was polarising. It opened debate but
also violent reactions. It was followed by many subsequent
legal decisions at various levels of the country, culminating recently in *Dobbs v Jackson*, in which a majority of the
Supreme Court of 2022 ruled that the interpretations in
Roe and some later cases were 'egregiously wrong from the
start'. Several justices on this very same court in 2022 suggested that their colleagues' opinion and criticism of *Roe*
was either 'hypocrisy' or a deeply worrying threat to more
of our constitutional rights in the US.[5]

This is the law's way of solving problems, but we need
something else; we need to weave a different kind of
fabric.[6]

So now let me take you to another battle zone and a
peaceful piazza in the middle of it. There was a small,
pop-up massage parlour in the deathly space of wartime
Iraq, in the International Zone of Baghdad, and it was
known as Dojo's Day Spa. It was a trailer home raised
on stilts and flanked by palm trees, like many of the

temporary buildings erected there at the time. Inside it felt very Brechtian because it was. A young woman from the Philippines who owned and ran this place was the Mother Courage figure, a woman coming to benefit from the war. I remember her face clearly as she smiled upon greeting me at the door.[7] A few bottles of American shampoo were proudly displayed on a small wall shelf behind her, the way they might have been in an East German hair salon in the 1970s. This was, after all, a spa in a war zone. There was another woman with her, and together they had travelled from Manila to set up shop. They sent the US dollars earned from each massage, each pedicure, back to their children in the Philippines. One of the women told me that she was hoping that, with this money, her son could eventually go to college. Maybe even in the United States, she said. And by massaging tired American soldiers after a gruelling and tense day of fighting, these women provided a mutual service; they took and they gave.

A sign on the wall said, Homemade Comfort Food, which they sold in addition to their massages. (There were no sexual services on offer here; it was not that kind of place.) In offering these comforts in the middle of a highly regulated and militarised environment, they were providing soldiers with momentary relief from the stress and alienation of international war.

I looked at the soldiers who came in there, into this piazza. I saw them relax with moisturising face creams carefully applied. Most knew one another, but others did not and got to know each other there. They could talk to the women about what was going on in their lives. They were not judged for hating the war, for wanting to go home. Or for wanting to stay. Rather, these women were a support structure, however minimally and temporarily. Surrogates for the platonic sensual pleasures of home life and comfort in peacetime: the feeling of children crawling on your back; of mum's warm, homemade chilli; and so forth. And it worked. What was this? Of course, in that it was an exchange of goods and services for mutual benefit, it was capitalism. But it was not without important, positive externalities, as economists call them: situations in which a third party, who is not part of the immediate exchange, benefits. The beneficiary can be another person, a group, or society more generally. In this case, perhaps it is the families of the soldiers, their friends, their colleagues. For amid the fraught and unstable environment of a war zone, two forces, troops and migrant workers, organically found a way to spontaneously cooperate—they were responsible for one another in this very limited space. Not unlike the Japanese piano bar on New York's East Side, where I once worked, this space allows for a kind of community, however transient and superficial and, dare I say, however gendered. Not unlike the psychiatrist's couch where one individual is paid to listen to the other, exchanges between buyer and seller result in something positive for those there and for others who are not. For among the soldiers who visited this space, there was a shared sense of self, emanating from a shared need: what Maria Montessori, the Italian paediatrician and educator, called care of oneself. Small, perhaps, and to some insignificant. But it is anything but. For in this place, in the middle of a war zone, some small sense of dignity was found, and the people who came in left a bit restored.

The scene in Baghdad is exactly what Michael Polanyi might have called spontaneous cooperation, even if it were based on self-interest. Cooperation needs trust, and trust needs a shared sense of values, and that shared sense can often be found initially through these piazza spaces.

Another example of this spontaneous order in a fixed place can be found very far from Baghdad, in the Bury Knowle Park in Oxford, where, on any given day in summer, Black, brown, and white children of different religions and classes can, and do, come together to unblock the water pump without parent or teacher or bully to interrupt the process. These young people actually behave much like the elderly men in a diner on the South Side of Chicago, where sociologist Mitchell Duneier studied race relations and documented these men in his award-winning book, *Slim's Table*. Duneier found that the key to the solidarity and consciousness of the Black men in this community rested in large part on the mutual respect and shared sense of identity of all the men in this space, across racial lines. There was a space for them to develop a sense of each other, repeatedly, on their own. They could choose when to be there, when not. They could talk over cheap coffee and find something to unite them, a sense of shared self, and they organised themselves spontaneously around that. Significantly, this small pocket existed as an island, on the South Side of Chicago, immortalized by Richard Wright's *Native Son*, *The Blues Brothers*, and Jim Croce's 'Bad, Bad Leroy Brown', as one of the most racially and ethnically mixed parts of the city (and the United States more generally), with a frighteningly large disparity between the haves and have-nots.

But let's remember what the bubbles showed us. Nature can find its own good order, if left to its own devices. And what these pockets in Chicago, Baghdad, and Oxford show us is that we will have the most opportunity to find our own good order when shared spaces, however small and makeshift, are created by and used regularly by us, qua community. A new understanding of a very old idea: the piazza—'an opening in the city fabric that allows public access and activity in various forms'.[8] With roots in the Greek agora, piazzas have been sites that vacillated through the centuries between state military and political use, religious use, commercial use, and spontaneous public use. I suggest we reclaim these special spaces—neither purely private nor state owned—as public spheres between the private and state nooks and crannies, which I call here the piazza.

The urban geographer David Harvey has often wondered about our 'places of sociality', as he calls them. In these places, Harvey suggests that differences can and should bump up against one another, and through this process, these iterations, we can 'work things out'.[9] It is a utopian idea, sure; for in some spaces, such differences, when allowed to bump up against one another, have actually led to violence. But this decentralised and spontaneous working out of our differences—and in this process, our recognition that in spite of these differences, we actually share some fundamental values—lies at the heart of my utopian project, too. For once we come together to understand the differences a little better, the rest will, hopefully, follow. But there will probably be a few bumps along the way.

Let's go back, for example, to the 1970s, in Notting Hill, west London, which was not that different from Chicago's South Side at the time. It was filled with dilapidated terraced houses, peppered by the occasional unreconstructed Second World War bomb site. The lack of council funding for this area made it an unsightly part of London and, therefore, a cheap source of housing. Unlike today, Notting Hill in the '70s drew London's less wealthy, many of them immigrants, who could not afford rents in the greener and cleaner parts of the city. Many of these immigrants were from former British colonies, and many Black families from the West Indies were among them. These families found comfort and community here, organising meeting places—their version of the piazza—where they could share the food, music, and culture they needed in order to properly imagine their own community alongside that of white Britain.

The Mangrove restaurant at number 8 All Saints Road, W11, was one such place. Open all night, with most of its trade happening after midnight, it drew a myriad of immigrants from Jamaica and other areas of the Caribbean who were now living in London: from unknown locals with young families to famous Black artists, intellectuals, and musicians. The site was managed by its owner, civil rights activist Frank Crichlow, but the spontaneous blossoming of a community hub around this restaurant was a very local, decentralised process, the culmination of which was the building of a real community—the community that would win one of the most important legal battles against racism in British history.[10]

London police repeatedly raided the Mangrove, claiming it was a source of drugs and prostitution. Locals denied these allegations, and proof of any illegal, antisocial behaviour was never found. After twelve police raids within the space of eighteen months, all in the name of finding evidence of illegal activity, frustrated locals decided together to form the Action Committee for the Defence of the Mangrove. On 9 August 1970, 150 members of this committee and other supporters from the neighbourhood marched on the local police station in Notting Hill to protest what they considered repeated police harassment based on racial hatred. The Metropolitan Police mobilised the Special Branch including plain-clothes officers and photographers, who mingled among the protestors. In what was later found to be a deliberate attempt by police to target the emerging Black Power movement, the 'heavy-handed' police infiltration incited violent clashes. In the aftermath, police arrested those who would become known as the Mangrove Nine—nine of the activists defending the restaurant—and charged them with incitement to riot, among other things.[11]

The nine arrested members demanded an all-Black jury, a jury of their peers. Following precedents set by the Black Panthers in the United States, these nine individuals and their supporters worked to build a network of information, elevating the case from a local example of racial clashes with police to one of critical national importance with implications for all nation-states around the world. Members of the Mangrove community distributed pamphlets and began a public education campaign to raise awareness of the case, and of institutional racism more generally. After fifty-five days of trial by jury, all nine were acquitted of the most serious charges against them; five were acquitted of all charges. The decision was a landmark one in a very critical sense: it was the first time a judge acknowledged both racial prejudice and wrongdoing in the London Metropolitan Police.[12] But the good work did not stop here.

With this decision, and the support and attention they had raised nationally, the Mangrove Nine disbanded, but then they and their community worked in different groups and organisations, like circles in a Venn diagram, to advance police reform and accountability in Britain over the next decades. Through new groups and movements, these overlapping circles of cooperation came and went and learned from each other. Further offshoots included the Mangrove Community Association, which became a kind of YMCA plus, aiming to provide services for the young and old members of the community and rehabilitate former prisoners. This shows how spontaneous, self-enforcing cooperation started locally, in a specific piazza, and then created enough immediate trust throughout a community to provide the basis for social interaction at a macro level.

I sent some questions over to the Mangrove Nine's official photographer, Jamaica-born Neil Kenlock. Kenlock, now in his seventies, documented the experience of these movements but also the Black experience in the United Kingdom more generally. I was curious about the way the movement that supported the Mangrove Nine was born, how it organised itself, who its leaders were—if any. Kenlock told me by email that, quite simply, 'there was no one to say you should be somewhere at 10 o'clock, people just looked at the situation and took action'. There was no dominating leadership, no hierarchy. People educated themselves. They brought in those who had more knowledge, more experience, to share their stories. This was inspiration and education, not mobilisation. Importantly, as Kenlock said, 'Nobody told them to do it, but they wanted to be involved.' Why? It was obvious. 'The people knew each other, and they understood. Each person was looking in the same direction.'[13] And this is the power of the piazza, for it makes it possible for us to look in the same direction, literally—and to get a shared sense of each other. In so doing, we can then take steps to coordinate our actions and make things happen, just as they did in Notting Hill.

Several years ago, my family took a day trip to a bucolic Oxfordshire village. Beyond the village school and its playground, towards the brambles and fields, a group of young boys, between the ages of about eight and fourteen, were all hard at work with shovels and spades, digging up a small plot on the edge of the playground that I at first thought might be a village gardening allotment. These boys were in fact not planting vegetables but creating hills for an off-road bike track, carving not only the main space but also the channelling side spaces, determining their own gradients and making that space their own. Working together, having outgrown the toddler swings and slide on the adjacent playground long ago, they were deciding what they wanted this sub-space place to be for them now and doing it. This is in many ways how a piazza begins.

Something pretty similar developed in Birmingham during the pandemic. The young people this time were a bit older but similarly motivated to make a public, open space for their sport at a time when indoor piazzas were off limits because of public health risks. Bournbrook

Skatepark in Birmingham was started during the dark, bleak days of 2020 in a city known for its social and economic diversity. Over the previous decades, citizens there had tried to manage this diversity via local government. In a world and a city suspicious of Islamic radicalisation, and not long after the highly contested allegations surrounding Islamic extremism in the city's schools, this was perhaps an unlikely place for such a community project to succeed.[14] But in spite of or maybe because of this diversity, within Birmingham, Bournbrook had seen waves of positive engagement over the past decades. It was one of the first public places in Europe where graffiti was legally allowed and even sometimes invited. Banksy and artists of varying degrees of notoriety had exhibited here. Yet some of the spaces, through the years, through the generational shifts that must and do happen, grew disused and tired and even dilapidated.

So, during COVID, a group of young skaters, frustrated by their own confinement and mindful of the waste of good useable spaces in the city, decided to do something about it. Together they spent thousands of hours pulling weeds and bramble, sweeping and clearing away debris, and then finding the right volunteers with construction skills to help create a community skatepark. All of this was temporarily blocked by the city council, but skaters negotiated their way out of the red-tape web. Their project has been so successful that the local council now supports the park. With local businesses also on board, together these various groups co-manage it. Adding to the success is how open this park is. Indoor skateparks charge entrance fees and therefore exclude those who cannot pay. Outdoor skateparks do not. Outdoor basketball courts and football pitches tend to be used by the athletic and male, but outdoor skateparks are the places where young people across races, genders, abilities, and age groups can come together and share something—their love of the sport and of the subculture that goes with it. That shared identity transcends other identities and creates the kind of bond necessary to cut across potentially divisive cleavages, such as race or religion or sometimes even gender. It is not without its challenges, to be sure. But it is in working out those challenges, through the piazza in whatever form, that citizens begin to understand both what makes them different from others and, more importantly, how much they have in common.[15]

Coming out of the pandemic, we know that the park and similar projects had at least twin effects on our communities and their spaces. (We are waiting to see how long they may last, but while they do, they provide eyes on the street and turn abandoned, blighted spaces into populous and loved ones. And they provide a basis for recovery not solely reliant on retail activities or leisure activities such as going to bars or dining. Which is to say, a basis that isn't simply spending money.) First, and quite clearly to all, the legal restrictions during lockdown led to increased use of private spaces, which has had momentum beyond the pandemic as we continue to appreciate more solitude and more distance. For with increased and more permanent calls for remote working, online learning, and telemedicine, having gone inside by necessity, some have decided to stay by choice. This clearly has some negative implications for our sociality. At least one research project led by the British Academy found that 'COVID-19 and the government response to it have impacted different people in different ways, often amplifying existing structural inequalities in income and poverty, socioeconomic inequalities in education and skills, and intergenerational inequalities—with particular effects on children'.[16] These inequalities may now make it ever more challenging for us to come together.

However, the second effect we have seen is exactly the one exhibited by skateboarders and other citizens who depend on these piazzas for their needs and lamented both their legal closure for public health reasons and that overwhelmed governments could no longer manage basic care of the infrastructure while they were closed by mandate. Here individuals and groups acted by making their own piazzas, from community gardens and food larders to skateparks—projects that in some cases were so important to the communities that they encouraged new thinking about what public space should be post-pandemic and how we should collectively imagine it.

The piazza: a hairdresser's, massage parlour, a local diner, the all-night bookshop-café, an outdoor community skatepark. Bowling together, not alone.[17] Being physically present in the public sphere, repeatedly, and getting to know the people in it in order to form a common bond, a sense of each other and a sense of the place itself.

That bond, more than any particular space, is my third pillar in our quest to become better, happier, more active citizens. It is not new. And some countries, such as the United States, were once actually rather good at building those bonds, at least for some of their people. So good that a visiting Frenchman, Alexis de Tocqueville, praised American associational life and suggested, enviously, that it was this unique characteristic that made American democracy work when no others seemed to be doing that well at all. Tables have certainly turned since the early 1800s. I don't know what Tocqueville might have thought of a community-built skatepark as a form of democratic, associational life, but I believe he would have been impressed. The multiple examples that proliferated during the pandemic demonstrate that the foundation is already there, if latent, in many specific cultures if not entire countries, no matter how divided we might be now. From these leisure projects, to the community orchards and gardens that sprang up across the world to help with food crises, we know that people crave these places, for public space is a teacher, and we have plenty to learn from it now after their long closure, as we look to the post-pandemic future of the piazza.

So, why is any of this important in my theory? Because rules cannot give us cooperation. The law does not encourage us or even force us to cooperate. This is not its goal. The piazza is the place for settling through cooperation, for forming a shared sense of self, for understanding what we have in common and what not, and sometimes that might involve conflict. Imagine for a moment standing in a long queue at the supermarket, where only one till is open and staff are standing around. You glance at the person in front of you, and behind. One of you begins to talk, mentioning that you are in a short-stay parking zone, that you need to pick up your child from school, that you wonder if they can simply open another till. As a few of you join the conversation, a member of staff overhears your discontent, or one of you—empowered by knowing that you share the feelings of others—bravely asks the staff to open another till. And they do. And you realise that they probably just needed a little nudge. This is the power of the piazza, even if in a very immediate, finite way.

The piazza works because it provides a space for common knowledge—for increasing the chances that you know, that someone else knows, that yet another person knows something. It sounds like a childhood riddle or tongue twister when stated this way: I know that you know that I know . . . and so on. But this is a fundamental concept in social science, and common knowledge is now believed to be at the heart of cooperation. Because when we try to cooperate, we will always have some coordination problems: where to meet, when to do so, how to get there, who does what—such challenges arise everywhere.

Think of trying to set up a play date in a public space for your child and two of her young friends. Or worse, getting a small group of relatives together for a birthday. Even in today's high-tech world, it's not easy. This simple fact—that coordination is complex and often a lack of it impedes cooperation—can be exploited by governments, particularly totalitarian governments, as a way of preventing protests and other types of collective action that are meant to challenge existing practices. Think for a moment about Cold War films which depicted life in Eastern Europe and the former Soviet space. One goal of the dictatorial regime was to stop common knowledge, to stop people from knowing that others were fed up with the regime and wanted to change it, from knowing that others knew this, and so on. Dictatorships thrive when they atomise people, because atomised people are usually weaker and do not know that others know that they know that they are all fed up and want change and are ready to do something about it—as long as they don't have to do it alone. When common knowledge does not exist, then the only knowledge is private knowledge, or it is not knowledge at all but a sort of fake news fabricated by the regime or its puppets or private interests. True democracy needs cooperation. Cooperation needs common knowledge. Common knowledge needs the piazza.

Michael Chwe, a game theorist and one of the important theorists of common knowledge, talked about an experiment done in Mexico:[18]

In partnership with the UNESCO office in Mexico, Eric Arias, a graduate student in political science at NYU, measured the effects of an anti-violence audio soap opera program in San Bartolome Quialana, a rural community in Oaxaca. Arias found that when a person listened to the soap opera on a CD player in his own home, it did not have a significant effect on his attitudes about violence against women. However, when the program was played over the village loudspeaker, or in community meetings, it did have an effect. In other words, the soap opera seemed to be effective only when it was common knowledge, when each person knew that other people heard it.[19]

Because when those hearing the anti-violence message in the public spaces could see that others were hearing it, too, they realised that others now knew that violence against women was problematic. So it was not only the content that mattered but the fact that people now knew that others had heard that important content, too. The idea that domestic violence was a horror was now common knowledge. Another example of the unique power of the piazza.[20]

Is there any evidence from another time or another space that suggests any of this really matters for democracy—for making our lives better in other ways? In the late 1980s, my former Harvard colleague Bob Putnam set out, with two Italian researchers, Robert Leonardi and Raffaella Nanetti, to study Italian democracy. Bob and his team were particularly interested in understanding the variation within one country in how 'democratic' different regions were. In the 1970s, the Italian government decided to decentralise itself, giving regions each legal autonomy in certain policy areas, as well as their own institutional infrastructure. Bob and his colleagues wanted to understand why, almost twenty years later, some of these regions were shining examples of democracy (efficient, accountable, effective at delivering public goods) while others were struggling to meet even basic criteria. What they found was striking: the success of democracy depended fundamentally not on the quality of the legislators or the institutions but rather on the horizontal bonds between citizens. Putnam referred to these bonds and the norms associated with these connections as social capital. Northern Italy was by far the strongest overachiever; what he and his team found was that this region had a stronger history of community engagement—of guilds and clubs, choral societies, and so forth—than its southern counterparts.[21]

Two caveats are in order. First, although these correlations are documented, we do not always fully understand the arrows of causation—meaning that there is always a chicken-and-egg problem with this kind of research. But a proven correlation is already pretty good. What's more, the preschool phenomenon that ignited educators' imaginations all over the world, one that I discuss later in detail, was born in the northern Italian city of Reggio Emilia, in Emilia-Romagna, the region in Putnam's research that outperformed all others. There is something in the idea that trust built up through social capital matters for the culture of democracy and its citizens in the long run.

The second caveat concerns the possible dangers of social capital, or let's call it the perversions of these social groups. Sheri Berman offered an important critique of the idea that civic associations, and in particular very organised groups, were a straight line to robust democracy, by showing that the Nazis in Germany, for example, targeted and infiltrated existing civic groups during the richly experimental and progressive Weimar period, using this dense network of social capital to further their fascist goals.[22] We do need to be wary of this. But the key to what I'd like to encourage is not so much hierarchical groups, like youth teams with high fees and competitive entry requirements, though voluntary youth and other groups can be enjoyable associations, but rather, the spontaneous meeting of people in the public sphere, where there is free entry and exit, where there are no dues or fees to pay, where leaders—if they exist at all—are mere facilitators or coordinators rather than directors or managers or captains, and where we come together of our own free will and know that we will not be required to be there, to show up, if we don't want to.

A half century ago, German philosopher Jürgen Habermas was one of the first to theorise what he referred to as the 'public sphere'. In a classic article, Habermas stated that 'by the "public sphere" we mean first of all a realm of our social life in which something approaching public opinion can be formed. Access is guaranteed to all citizens.'[23] The postwar German theorists, Habermas principally among them, were aware and accepting of the failures of Marxist theories to provide realistic paths forward. The Berlin Wall going up, however, did not completely negate the intellectual project—the critiques of capitalism in Karl Marx's work and his work with Friedrich Engels. Many theorists disagreed vehemently with the political embodiment that Marxism took in the Soviet Union and Eastern Europe at that time but wondered whether something could be salvaged from the work that Marx began. So the Frankfurt school, this loose group of intellectuals who hoped to rescue some seeds of Marxist thought and make them more applicable to the then-pressing postwar concerns, understandably wanted to spend less thought on the political classes and politicians and more on the power of the public sphere, of ordinary citizens engaging with one another in these free spaces to generate thoughts, critiques of the ruling classes, and even programmes for a better, more equitable, and democratic future.

But these philosophers, even Habermas himself, noted the real challenges of getting an ideal, true public sphere— in particular, the requirement that 'access is guaranteed to all citizens'. To understand the emphasis on 'all', we need only think of women and minorities, of those with physical or mental conditions, of all those who are not able to freely access the public sphere and who, consequently, lose out on the important, the necessary, process of social life in which something approaching public opinion can be formed.

The internet and social media have made an important contribution, if a qualified one, not without commercial and other private interests and control, to opening up the public sphere to all of us. But what we still need more than anything now as we come out of the pandemic of 2020 is a genuine face-to-face public space, a piazza, in which access is not only theoretically but also realistically, concretely, guaranteed to all.

What are these spaces going to look like in 2024 and beyond? They cannot, must not, be the exclusionary spaces that have kept certain genders or races, certain groups, excluded from participation, either formally or practically. We pretty much acknowledge now that some of our most precious historical spaces cannot be accessed by those in a wheelchair, those who find cobblestones difficult to cross on foot. There is no other option if our spaces have these physical barriers to entry.

And what of the invisible cobblestones? We have to think of others, those who, because they are neurodivergent, find some spaces overwhelming; have infants or young children and so need quiet pockets in public spaces to breastfeed; are transgender and do not want to be stared at or ridiculed or made to feel odd in public; are financially insecure with little time for leisure; or are otherwise unable to even get out of their homes or workplaces to meet. All of these situations create barriers to entry to the public sphere, and the burden is on us to create the open piazzas that we will all be able to frequent; the burden is on us to think about how we can increasingly make leisure time a necessary part of the day for all. Not the kind of conspicuous or visible leisure that Thorstein Veblen was, rightly or wrongly, concerned about in the late 1800s—the wasteful consumerism that he claimed was not really leisure at all but pursuit of social prestige—but the leisure that allows us to both appreciate our differences and find literal and figurative common ground.[24]

So even getting to the piazza can be problematic and exclusionary, and it is here that we need to do more work and generate new ideas. Apoorva Tadepalli, a journalist from Bombay, commented:

> There is infrastructural exclusion through the public transit stations and schedules, designed for the non-disabled nine-to-five commuter who is not pregnant and does not make stops at the grocery store or daycare along the way. Women also incur the pink tax, relying more than men on public transportation and spending more per month on it, especially if they are primary caregivers. And then there's psychological exclusion: Women must factor the fear of being attacked into their daily routine as they move through public spaces, which takes a mental toll (and perhaps an economic one, for the safety of taking a taxi or living in a building with security).

She was reviewing the work of Leslie Kern, a feminist urban scholar from Toronto who is trying to get us to understand both the overt and covert, deliberate and non-deliberate ways that our cities and spaces discriminate and exclude, and therefore are anything but democratic.[25]

Kern is, thankfully, not the only one helping us open up the piazzas—spiritually or literally. Architects and scholars of public health and geography and urban planning are also now coming together to design what is being called 'trauma-informed neighbourhoods'. These are public spaces whose designers look carefully at the physical aspects of the neighbourhood—'lighting, traffic density, noise, and green space'—and try to document the harm to both physical and mental health but also to think about how specific neighbourhood designs can either trigger trauma or promote healing, and they are finding ways to build more of the latter.[26]

If you are a stay-at-home parent, you need at least some time in the day to leave your home and get to the piazza, safely and in a way that works for your kids; if you work as a nanny during the day and then clean office buildings at night, we need to make it possible for you to participate in associational life as well. For the harsh distinction between the private and public spheres has for so long assumed an unrealistic conception of the piazza: white men enjoying leisure time. This is a lot of what Tocqueville saw and loved. But today's Tocqueville—that great lover of equality—would surely see it now as a good start but also an imbalanced, uneven, and unhealthy state of affairs, for our public spheres and our associational life will never fully thrive until all have access, until all have been given the capabilities necessary for participation.[27]

In terms of practical steps we can take, we should look at Kern and the other important work that is increasingly being done by geographers, urban planners, and landscape architects who care about access. Take, as another example, the work of Elizabeth Sweet, a geographer who thinks that we might reduce violence in city spaces by linking, rather than separating, the public and private spheres—actually blurring the divide between them. Radically different in a way from the post–Frankfurt school project which separated them to protect associational life, this idea fuses the spheres. The private sphere is arguably at the heart of many problems today, including the continued subjection of women but also of LGBTQ+ people; it is still the default space of some disabled people, or of any minority that feels, if not legally then emotionally or otherwise, excluded from the public sphere. The stay-at-home mum or dad with no free time. The young man with chronic fatigue syndrome who can't easily get out of bed. The autistic teenager who fears social interaction. So Sweet calls for urban planning that actually focuses on the private parts of us, our bodies and emotions, as a point of departure. This is embodied citizenship. It makes sense, because we know that physical and emotional safety is obviously critical to the community (to the public space), and we also know that this safety has a direct feedback effect on the individual person's physical body and mind (the private space). For Sweet, then, these areas are absolutely related in a reciprocal and dynamic fashion—and so why artificially keep them apart? Thinking through an urban space for Sweet then includes thinking about the urban emotion, and any attempts to help create what I would call piazzas would need to consider ways to allow for true participation but also the capacity for the spaces to absorb and mediate emotions as a way of blending the private and public, of making them more continuous because we make these spaces feel more comfortable and welcoming.[28] A new kind of body politic, an embodied one. Clearly, we need to know and think and discuss this together to figure out how this might practically be done.

But we have some ideas of where and how we might start. During our absence from the piazzas during the pandemic, we all suffered, as data demonstrates the sharp increase in physical and mental health problems directly related to our isolation.[29] But when we did return to these places and spaces, especially our outdoor piazzas, we had an astounding appreciation for what had changed. Pollution decreased, biodiversity increased. Bird species began to use tonal mating calls that had not been heard for decades owing to noise from traffic and industry, and residents in parts of India could, for the first time in decades, see the Himalayas from their rooftops. All of this motivated us to return to our spaces, but differently. We began thinking more about light and light pollution; we began thinking more about how our senses had been overwhelmed by our public spaces, rather than nourished by them.

Take sound—or the lack of it. The great French historian of the senses, Alain Corbin, noted that centuries ago, 'The intimacy of places, that of the bedroom and its furniture, like that of the house, was bound up with silence.'[30] Indeed, silence—and all that it entails, not only the absence of noise—may be the place to start. Not by prohibiting noise but by trying to recapture something of the intimacy of the private sphere, transporting it to the public one. What our return to the piazzas after the pandemic has shown us is that we can work with urban planners and local governments to create a living public museum of silence, where various intimate pockets of our own private selves can feel welcome and comfortable in the public sphere, comfortable enough to be shared and experienced together. Corbin makes an exquisitely written plea: 'My evocation in this book of the silence of the past and of how people searched for it, and of the qualities, disciplines, tactics, richness and power of the speech of silence, may help us to relearn how to be silent, that is, to be ourselves.'[31] And how can we do this? Maybe the fifteen-minute city, one of the hottest and most controversial ideas today, is a place to begin.

The fifteen-minute city is an idea made popular recently by Carlos Moreno, the French Colombian urban planner, who lamented the fact that we were constantly being asked to adapt to an urban infrastructure that meant walking and biking less to get our basic needs met. From shopping to seeing doctors to finding a playground, we were getting into cars or avoiding these trips altogether, and this was causing the piazza to vanish.

What Moreno proposed, and cities from Paris to Seattle have tried to implement, was to make most of the urban dweller's needs available to them within a radius of fifteen-minute travel time.

How do you accomplish it? Well, for one, you use and reuse spaces that already exist, but in an off-label sort of way. Creatively, school playgrounds remain open after school, to provide spaces for the community to use for other activities or events. So instead of ushering parents off the school grounds at 3 p.m. when school is finished for the day, parents and their children are allowed or even encouraged to stay. Maybe the space becomes a tai chi area for city-sponsored classes. Maybe elderly residents are invited to walk around the grounds for exercise. The point for Moreno is to make use of what is already there, for the spaces themselves to multi-task. What we need to do is also encourage these piazzas to look more like the ancient ones, with less traffic and less noise but more of the right sound—the sound of people talking, playing, living as their true selves.

Moreno, in a 2020 TED Talk, said that only three elements are critical to starting us down the path of the fifteen-minute city. First, Moreno says cities must be made for humans, not for cars. Second, every square metre in the city needs to be used for multiple things; it should not serve only one purpose. And three, the neighbourhood needs to be arranged in such a way that residents can live, work, and thrive without commuting. This doesn't mean of course that people cannot or should not travel or go out of their immediate spaces if they wish to. It is not meant to create an enclave, a cult-like commune, which builds walls to keep people in and outsiders out. We are not returning to the medieval walled city, even if we are looking to history for our inspiration. These elements undoubtedly need supportive infrastructure to work, and this is where local governments and their budgets and planning boards can be of help.

Aristotle suggested that politics was essential to the development of good citizens, because he believed that through our participation in the polis, we developed our character in such a way that made us good—good in that we had civic virtue, a specific kind of well-meaning attitude towards our fellow citizens that, in the words of Michael Sandel, 'we can't develop at home'.[32] I'm going to close this chapter by suggesting here a critical nuance: that it is exactly the kind of civic virtue that we want and need to develop, but that it can and must develop 'at home'— where home is neither the private house nor the world of electoral politics but that public sphere between the two that I have here called the piazza and which, in many ways, is and should be 'political'.

Evidence is already showing us how it works. For even before the pandemic, sociologists and criminologists set out to study one of the cities most cited in the United Kingdom for high crime rates, Sheffield, once a very noisy city and the heart of steel production during the Industrial Revolution. They wanted to see whether there was any significant variation among the various neighbourhoods, and if so, what explained the 'overachievers'—the neighbourhoods that, in spite of the usual factors that tended to lead to high crime, were actually doing fairly well. A budget cut at one point in time that meant less state investment in infrastructure including the police offered an important opportunity for these researchers to observe whether any of the groups living in this complex city were 'resilient'.[33] Not unlike in Kerala, some many miles and cultures away, or San Francisco or Chicago, the researchers found that there was indeed variation. And factors that were most offered as important for helping groups have a sense of themselves and a desire to progress were public community spaces. This includes both green outdoor community areas and indoor community centres but, important and common to both, locations where there was less social and environmental destruction and instead a greater sense of security—security in all its meanings.[34] So the safe piazza was critical, for it was here that individuals could meet face to face and exchange ideas and get a sense of one another in ways that were important not only for leisure and physical and mental health but also for safe citizenship.

So go ahead, hang out in a piazza, repeatedly. Take a friend or neighbour with you. Or meet a new friend there, and see just what you can do. If we do this, we increase our chances of moving away from hierarchy and leadership by getting into these spaces and just being, which will give us an embodied citizenship—one that actually engages our sensory and motor systems.[35] For the law can contain us, it can tell us what our leaders think is right and wrong. But let's remember its adversarial nature, its violence: for as the legal scholar Austin Sarat says, 'Law depends on violence and uses it as a counterpunch to the allegedly more lethal and destructive violence situated just beyond law's boundaries. But the violence on which law depends always threatens the values for which law stands.'[36] We do not need more violence, of any kind, in our democracies.

This chapter has been about the cooperative spaces of citizenship, how to get to them, how to make them work for us, and how to simply realise what potential they contain when we find ourselves there, naturally. The next chapter is about the projects that can come out of our time in these spaces, spontaneously, and the projects that can also, reciprocally, bring us back to these spaces over and over again. So that everyone does know your name.

CHAPTER FIVE

Grow Your Own Tomatoes, and Share Them

Iɴ ᴛʜᴇ ꜱᴇᴍɪ-ᴀʀɪᴅ ᴄᴏᴜɴᴛʀʏꜱɪᴅᴇ ᴏꜰ ꜱᴏᴜᴛʜᴡᴇꜱᴛᴇʀɴ France, about an hour's drive from the Hexagon's fastest growing city, Montpellier, I met a middle-aged French couple, Frédéric and Dominique, who have built what they consider to be a political project. It is an experiment in permaculture on a vast, uninhabited plot of very dry land. Incorporating innovative technology but also relying on ancient principles, they are hoping to return to what they and many note is the original Greek understanding of 'human': of the earth.

Frédéric's discussion reminded me that according to Greek mythology, the Titan god Prometheus created humanity from clay, from the earth itself. Stealing fire from the gods and giving it to humans, he empowered people to take care of themselves and their fellow human beings. Frédéric and Dominique's project, which remains spontaneous and loosely defined, seeks to encourage a system of self-sustaining, environmentally protective structures that nurture both the land and a community of visitors and educators, promoting self-sufficiency on one hand and healthy codependence on the other. Using solar and hydroelectric power to grow food and heat buildings, this space aims to become not isolated but experimentally self-sufficient, gaining its independence from both the state and private industry. Their swimming pool is not manufactured and imported, with the large carbon footprint that comes with that kind of product, but a hole carved into the ground, where naturally forming algae serves as its filtration system. Swimming in it, I felt its emerald-green water surround me, as my body began to appreciate the clean, chlorine-free water. Gazing at the vast sky, my family and I felt a connection to the earth that was, quite frankly, grounding. From here, from this commitment to and respect for space and its lack of materialism but heavy materiality, we begin to open our minds to the kind of solidarity and self-sufficiency that means something for the spontaneous orders we need. Here I began to imagine a world in which we ourselves embrace these principles of self-sufficiency to address the twin problems of food scarcity and environmental ruin.

The law does not yet tell us how to be self-sufficient, particularly in these critical areas that are so immediate to our daily lives—food and the natural world around us. The law's point is not really to encourage our independence, so how could we expect it to encourage us to grow our own food and to share it? To be sure, there is an increasingly important area of law we know as environmental law, as peoples around the globe begin to craft new laws to protect the earth and take corporations and governments to court to hold them accountable for policies and practices that violate environmental principles. These are important applications of the law, ones I am not going to pretend are useless. In fact, this may be one critical area where laws can be used by citizens, if citizens are made aware of them. When, to give an example, the Godawari Marble Industries was told by the Supreme Court of Nepal that a clean and healthy environment was definitely a part of the right to life guaranteed in the constitution of Nepal, the company had to listen, and legislation soon followed with an Environmental Protection Act.[1] While this was an important step, both practically and symbolically, for individual health and the environment, the Supreme Court of Nepal tried to balance its criticism of Godawari Marble by stating that this industry was fundamental to the Nepalese economy. It is often in this delicate balancing act that individuals and their rights, such as the right to food and to clean, sustainable living, can get lost. And if the law and courts tip too far in favour of large-scale industry to the detriment of our health and the health of our environment, the perversions in our reliance on law and courts to do the work for us show in sad detail.

Here's what I mean. A few years ago, I travelled to northern Italy to work with Alex Majoli, a Magnum war photographer. Under his direction, I wanted to carve a visual ethnography of law's perversion, so I set out with my camera early one cold November morning to take pictures of—dairy cows. Because these particular cows were producing milk, like any other dairy herd, but milk that would be distributed via vending machines in towns and villages, with twenty-four-hour access. This was not the 7-Eleven or the all-night Tesco run by large corporations: it was a system through which local farmers delivered their milk to sterile vats, so that individuals could come with their own bottles and fill them up, so even if you needed milk in the middle of the night, you could find it. And, most interestingly of all, it was *raw*, unpasteurised milk, a taboo in several parts of the world.

Fascinated by this, I set out to take the photos: of the cows, the farmers, of the machines and the people who used them. I accompanied one farmer to the vending machines as she refilled them after a long morning taking care of young calves. The directness of this form of product delivery, where the supply chain was extremely short, was tremendously interesting to me, particularly because local authorities sanctioned this kind of self-sufficiency.

Later that day, returning to our photography workshop, Alex and his staff at the Cesuralab seemed mildly amused. We had been given several bottles of raw milk by these generous farmers and enjoyed them with hot tea while looking at our day's work. But why, they asked, was I so taken with this? Because, I told them, in the United States, where I come from, raw milk is prohibited by law in many states—it is believed to be a health risk. It can be risky: if farmers are not careful with their production, are not clean and do not test their animals regularly, milk-borne illnesses through bacterial contamination can pose a public health problem. Many states mandated pasteurisation, with various changes and exceptions since the early 1900s. So today, in some parts of the United States, this delicious raw milk that we were enjoying with our tea was more difficult to buy than a handgun. US states listed in 2022 as having the least restrictive gun laws but where selling raw milk is prohibited by law include Alabama, West Virginia, Wyoming, Georgia, Alaska, North Dakota, and Kentucky. This is how the law in areas related to food and the environment could be perverse. And when it comes to helping people take care of their health and the health of the earth, to being self-sufficient in these critical areas, the law seems to be far behind.[2]

The economist Scott Nearing created his own approach, his own Walden, in Maine, where he practised and preached rural homesteading and invited others to learn it, too.[3] In the United Kingdom, John Seymour did much of the same, teaching us to nurture the land, and nurture ourselves; to take responsibility for the environment, and for our own food; to return to values that include simplicity and a different idea of having enough. And most recently, perhaps the most salient of all for us now, Leah Penniman has created an eighty-acre organic farm in New York—Soul Fire Farm—based on what she terms 'silvo-pasture', a unique form of permaculture which respects the environment. The farm produces goods that are donated to the racially complex 'food deserts' around Albany and educates and encourages farmers of colour to embrace food sovereignty—a key step, she and others believe, in the fight for racial justice. Indeed. Leah starts with a simple statistic: 98 per cent of the land in the United States that can grow food is 'white owned'.[4] How can this be fair, in a country where—as of 2020—white people made up only 62 per cent of the entire population?

Rewilding is a close cousin of permaculture that has, especially since the pandemic, taken hold across many countries in rural pockets—but also within cities. A former farm in Sussex that once tried antibiotics and semi-industrial farm techniques to sustain its agriculture took a decision to return the land to its 'wild' state. Described by its owner, Isabella Tree, in her recent memoir, the land has been restored to a wild, unkept state, where now rare but important native species of plants and animals thrive—and are arguably in closer harmony with other native species, including us, than those previously raised and cultivated for industry.[5] But these projects, however important for the climate and romantically idyllic, have also met with resistance and conflict—sometimes based on critically important, real concerns. There is resistance from farmers who believe this land was meant to be used to produce food for local communities in real time, not for our hunter-gatherer ancestors. Resistance from those who think that leaving good land alone caters to the wealthy, when underprivileged peoples need housing and cost-efficient foods, not overpriced organic rare-breed meats. Indeed, the balance between what might be good for the environment and what is needed immediately to take care of the current population and address food scarcity is a difficult one to strike.

Perhaps the most enlightened of the self-sufficient farmers, homesteaders, and rewilding gurus, those who see themselves as custodians of the land past-present-future, meet at a central intersection, one that can be used as a point of departure for finding equilibrium: they are united in their desire to use their own resources, and often the resources of the local community, to provide for this local community and, in so doing, protect the land and all its creatures—including but not limited to us humans.

Self-sufficiency to address food scarcity and protect the environment does not subscribe to industrial farming, nor does the rewilding movement of Great Britain, the United States, and other countries. Both resist what they see as uninformed and short-sighted policies that complicate or demonise their efforts to respect the land, its natural capacity, and its inhabitants—human and non-human. And both have an understanding of individual and collective action that takes citizens seriously and hopes that the citizens may, in a future iteration of our world, be empowered to think and act for the collective good so as not to depend on multinational supermarket chains and global corporate interests. In the end, basically, they care about the future of our kids.

This kind of self-sufficiency is not meant to be the isolating, individualist survivalist approach to living that requires you to ignore your community and your state and look after only yourself. Instead, what I am suggesting is the kind of self-sufficiency that incorporates insights from early theorists of international trade, and here David Ricardo and John Stuart Mill come to mind. These theorists suggested a simple but powerful idea: comparative advantage—the idea that nations should trade with one another for mutual benefit concentrating on the areas in which they respectively have natural advantages. This should be the basis for our self-sufficiency. It is not the astronaut Mark Watney growing potatoes for his own survival on Mars, though even Mark worked to his advantage and grew the only thing that he could grow. This idea is instead about us deliberately connecting with others and trading with them in a horizontal way, seeking not profit from our exchanges but mutual care and feeding, and allowing the kind of natural redistribution that can happen when we grow our own food and have surplus that can benefit someone else.

Think of *Gilligan's Island*, the American sitcom that began with a simple premise: seven individuals from very different walks of life are marooned on a desert island, individuals who have to learn not only how to get along with one another but how to develop and make use of this idea of comparative advantage in order to survive. When I studied economics as an undergraduate, examples from popular culture were sometimes invoked to explain various concepts. Imagine a diverse group of exaggerated stereotypes who do not necessarily like one another or have anything in common but their fate—an aloof millionaire and his precious wife; a nerdy, nervous professor; a glamorous movie star; a down-to-earth farm girl; and of course the skipper and the lovable Gilligan—each with a different level of skill and intelligence, each with a distinct and often challenging personality, but, together, resourceful enough to survive and even be somewhat happy on this tiny island in the middle of the Pacific Ocean. It's an allegory for the way we must understand our lives. For the most part, and increasingly today, we live in communities that are at least as diverse in terms of not only personality and intelligence and skill set but also race, religion, ethnicity, and so forth. That's obviously true. But the challenges of crossing these barriers are real and solutions much less clear, as I explore in the next chapter, on 'ethnic food'. And yet they are increasingly important for the kind of cooperation that crosses cleavages and aims to build a strong community not in spite of but taking advantage of critical differences. This is the kind of community that, research tells us, is likely to be robust and resilient.[6] Gilligan and his marooned motley crew were encouraged by necessity; they had no one else to rely on, no state, no government, no corporations.

Fortunately, we are not in such a precarious position, but we have let the state, government, and corporations in existence hinder our efforts to create and sustain life together in a more horizontal way. In 2021, investigative journalists at the *Guardian* and Food & Water Watch published a damaging report, claiming that our so-called food choices were basically an illusion. They documented why and how 'a few powerful transnational companies dominate every link of the food supply chain: from seeds and fertilizers to slaughterhouses and supermarkets to cereals and beers'. What's more, as if that weren't enough, 'at least half of the 10 lowest-paid jobs are in the food industry. Farms and meat processing plants are among the most dangerous and exploitative workplaces' in the United States, the country studied.[7] Law exists to help regulate these sectors, but lawmakers do not necessarily have our overall best interests in mind when they tackle these industries. Let's remember how, during the onrush of the pandemic, then-president Donald Trump 'signed an executive order . . . compelling meat processors to remain open to head off shortages in the nation's food supply chains, despite mounting reports of plant worker deaths due to Covid-19'. He did this by using the law, invoking the Defense Production Act to classify meat plants as 'essential infrastructure'.[8] This was seen by many as a collaboration between the large meatpacking industries and government, one that used the law to protect business while putting the health and safety of workers and the wider population at risk.[9] Laws concerning food in many countries are yet to free themselves of their ties to powerful industrial lobbies and tend to focus on supporting and regulating mass production; what we need instead is food security through empowering individuals and communities and protecting the land itself.

Around the world, projects moving away from our dependence on food industries and their corporate suppliers, as well as the laws that regulate and protect them, are returning to the idea of working horizontally, locally, and directly with the land. Frustrated with the lack of access to green spaces, with food inequality and rising food prices, with the disuse of private and public land wasting away in the wake of government indecision or corporate control, people have begun multiple projects without waiting for governments to act. Many offer a kind of community gardening for the benefit of locals, one that takes advantage of ancient ideas of homesteading but again shares and cooperates rather than isolates. One such place currently in development is the Cutteslowe Community Orchard in Oxfordshire. This historically fascinating suburb is attested in the Doomsday Book of 1086, recorded with various medieval spellings, all of them unpronounceable to the outsider. Once a prehistoric burial mound, and much later the place where (in the 1930s) nine-foot spiked walls were built to divide the less wealthy social housing tenants from the wealthier, private landowners, Cutteslowe is now the site of unique community projects that took off during the pandemic, although they struggle to stay alive. Edible Cutteslowe defines itself as an informal group that 'is all about growing vegetables and fruit sustainably and locally. In the process, we hope to build community and have fun. It's simple. You grow some vegetables or fruit that you invite other people to forage.'[10] Working with the local primary school, the community centre, and a pop-up food bank for those who find themselves short of even basic food and supplies, the Cutteslowe Community Larder, the project aims to weave a support network throughout the community. And its beginning was so simple. Here a group of residents decided to come together in 2020 to rewild some of the community land in their pocket of North Oxford and make it, eventually, an edible work in progress. Reaching out to neighbours through social media, including Nextdoor, which is how I found it, the group invites locals to show up at this piazza regularly to help clear the land and plant and care for fruit trees that could be accessed by anyone in the community who wants, or needs, a bite of fruit or a chat with a neighbour or both.

Sure, you might say, that's a nice middle-class pocket with the luxury of green space and time to spare, in one of the wealthiest and greenest parts of the United Kingdom. True, sort of. In fact, many of the participants are working parents without much time to spare. It is, however, a small community on the outskirts of a wealthy city, so what about doing this in a much bigger and more complex place, a large city, a metropolis? And sharing it across this larger space as well? When the Guggenheim Museum in New York opened its main 2020 show, *Countryside: The Future*, in the midst of the pandemic, the museum made a decision to grow cherry tomatoes in a sustainable way on Fifth Avenue—a symbolic sign of life and growth in a time plagued by death and stagnation. As the *New York Times* noted, 'The tomatoes, housed in what looks like a radioactive shipping container on the sidewalk, were on view as part of the exhibition for just three weeks before the city folded in on itself. But they're still growing, their vines snipped every Tuesday and donated to City Harvest, at least a hundred pounds at a time.'[11]

This artistic demonstration continued to feed less fortunate New Yorkers and in so doing created a series of networks, important backward and forward linkages of cooperation that continue past the changing of the museum walls. The next step would be to reproduce this: more of these tomato experiments and more examples like it across other areas of agriculture, or textiles, or even IT. Kids from the city schools can get involved early, and a network of local cooperation that replicates itself, that sows seeds for its regeneration, spontaneously in the city is born. Obviously, those who come together to grow and share tomatoes are likely to have at least some similar values, similar ideas about what the world is and should be, similar ideas about what a good life should look like. Before long, more people, across other lines which might have otherwise divided them, also join in and find unity in a set of immediate common goals even if not all values align. The community remains both diverse and united, and so thrives. And while it might be tomatoes today, it might be something else tomorrow.

These places become micro-worlds that we can make for ourselves, using comparative advantage in our communities, to begin to provide for one another and ourselves. It was perhaps no accident that the Villeneuve complex I mentioned earlier, in which neighbours came together to save boys from a deadly fire, had a history before this, for it was a critical experiment in popular urbanism, a kind of urban workshop idea that came out of the May '68 movement in France. Activists, educators, architects, and artists there, from various races and backgrounds, stood up for their rights—particularly regarding housing and education. Activists, including the teacher André Béranger, his wife, Ariane, and neighbours, formed citizens' associations, producing their own newspapers and creating residents' round tables to which members of local government were invited and strongly encouraged to show up and participate, so that local policy could be made with the citizens, not just for them. In fact, their motto became 'that which is done for the inhabitants, without them, is often done against them'.[12]

And there is also evidence that this kind of self-sufficiency and unorganised organising can weave an important, supportive fabric throughout even the most godforsaken cities on earth. In the 1970s, two prominent architects, Dutchman Rem Koolhaas and Nigerian Kunlé Adeyemi, set out to see what happens to a society when the state is absent. They looked to Lagos and saw that the state had really withdrawn from the city, left it to its own devices, both in terms of money and services. But to their great surprise, the vacuum left by the failed state had been filled by 'an unbelievable proliferation of independent agency: each citizen needed to take, in any day, maybe 400 or 500 independent decisions on how to survive that extremely complex system. . . . [I]t was the ultimate dysfunctional city—but actually, in terms of all the initiatives and ingenuity, it mobilized an incredibly beautiful, almost utopian landscape of independence and agency.'[13] It is no coincidence that the Guggenheim's tomato-growing show was mainly curated by Koolhaas, and that it had set its sights more broadly than Manhattan sidewalks: it examined not only Lagos but other efforts to find alternative models to top-down, higher-law-driven societies. The show, which went up pre-COVID-19, was at first met with bemusement by city-dwelling critics; however, since its opening to the broader public, it has been increasingly seen as important and prescient.

Self-sufficiency is rarely studied by constitutional or legal scholars. For if we think about what the constitution is doing, we see that it is setting up a structure for a state and a certain vertical dependence between us and those who provide for us. But that dependence can also be the kind of iron cage that the sociologist Max Weber thought a lot about, and worried about, too. Law, and the bureaucracy that supports it, is rational and controlling—and that is why, in part, our climate is losing the battle, why we didn't protect ourselves early enough from COVID, and so forth. So my telling you all this in this chapter is my way of suggesting where and how we might move out of the iron cage, not into an irrational and inefficient world but into a more humane one.

Interestingly, several examples of self-sufficiency historically, across time and space, emerge from peoples who believe that their rights were being violated by unjust practices, either deliberate government law and policy or the unequal effects of a capitalist system, or both. The Freedom Farm Cooperative founded by activist Fannie Lou Hamer in the late 1960s in Mississippi was an attempt to help African Americans gain more political freedom by addressing economic dependence *first*. Her project and others that followed saw tides of success and failure but continue to this day as people recognise the inevitable link between food security, self-sufficiency, and civil and political rights. And this is how addressing food security links to other aspects of being a citizen, because the backward and forward linkages of being self-reliant both require horizontal community engagement and provide a basis for responsible rights ownership. The Montgomery bus boycott began in Alabama in 1955, when individual African American citizens pooled resources, including their cars, and organised themselves to ensure there was transport without the buses: a highly effective shadow economy evolved, one that allowed pressure on the bus companies to mount. Self-sufficiency, in the form of self-organised transport, provided a viable substitute for segregationist bus companies, but it did more than get people to work: it also helped support a rights revolution. So, now, too with land and food which are, in the words of Leah Penniman, 'salient' to protecting our rights, to liberation.[14]

The Granby Four Streets is a micro-neighbourhood near Prince's Park in Liverpool, a historic urban park designed and built in the mid-1800s.[15] The four streets—Beaconsfield Street, Cairns Street, Jermyn Street, and Ducie Street—are made up of mostly Victorian terraced housing and became a settling space for immigrants from the Commonwealth after the Second World War. This area, the Granby Four, as the streets, as well as surrounding roads, became known, gradually saw a rich mosaic of ethnicities move in and a flourishing of economic activity, as in other pockets of large European cities filled with interesting and productive immigrants from former colonies of the respective metropole. But the economic decline of Britain in the 1970s brought tough times throughout the United Kingdom, in particular to these streets, where unemployment skyrocketed and deprivation fuelled ethnic tensions and subsequent battles with police and law enforcement. Several of the iconic Victorian properties here were abandoned or their residents evicted, and so began a downward slide as derelict buildings contributed to a gradual but generalised decline of this once thriving, experimental micro-neighbourhood.

The buildings were eventually designated by the local council and government as a site for demolition and development, the twin Ds that often take over when community moves out and developers move in. Years of planning and meetings, and mixed efforts by local government, met with more years of resistance from locals who felt caught between government 'objectives' and the reality of empty, derelict housing. Then something great happened. Members of the community just began acting on their own. Residents of the roads started their own version of an urban rewilding project, painting or fixing up some of the run-down buildings, turning the disgraced and abandoned spaces into something the community could finally use. Perhaps because of a combination of their own paralysis and the movement and the action of local doers, the council eventually agreed to transfer ownership of these buildings to the residents, who formed an association; and with the help of several organisations, including the architectural firm Assemble, they turned the once-derelict Victorian terraced houses of the Granby Four into an award-winning winter garden, in which community members congregate: a true piazza, complete with a gardener in residence. In 2014, Assemble was awarded the United Kingdom's prestigious Turner Prize for their work in helping to build this true piece of living art—a work of art that was really the product of self-sufficient residents who simply grew tired of waiting for the government and local council to help them save their crumbling neighbourhood.

'A resourceful, creative group of residents started to bring the neighbourhood back to life by clearing, planting, painting, and campaigning. In 2011 they entered into an innovative form of community land ownership, the Community Land Trust, to secure 10 empty houses, and renovate them as affordable homes.'[16] This is how Assemble described their shared vision and work with these residents. A new self-sufficiency. For rewilding is relative—and it does not only mean bringing something back to its uncultivated state; it can arguably also mean a restoration of place that is respectful of the built environment, of history, and of the cultural memory of a space—if that cultural memory was indeed supportive of man and woman and beast in all their combinations and diversity.

And you might yourself already imagine the forward linkages that are possible here from this kind of self-sufficiency of food and land security. Scott Nearing and other proponents certainly claimed that their way of life led to better health and less need for medical doctors. Their account was personal and anecdotal. But more recently, researchers have accumulated evidence that shows substantial benefits. For example, a fascinating treatise entitled simply *Rewilding*, published by Cambridge University Press in 2019, collected evidence across fields, noting 'benefits provided by nature in cities include environmental or ecosystem services like heat mitigation, pollution reduction, drinking water and stormwater protection'.[17] But more specifically, the study details the evidence for 'cognitive and psychological benefits from having access to nature' which 'include stress reduction and increased capacity for attention', as well as physical health benefits which 'include improved immune function, increased physical activity, reduced cardiovascular morbidity, and improved pregnancy outcomes'.[18] We sort of knew that, or at least felt it. But what these researchers have done is show direct links between the land stewardship projects, community gardens, and rewilding projects in urban spaces and improved mental and physical health. So, yes, Nearing was right, and we might never figure out the exact, precise causation, whether it is the increased contact with nature or with other people or the sense of accomplishment or purpose or spirituality that causes better health, because they are feedback loops which are constantly supporting all elements. But what we do know is that these projects definitely result in better health for both the active and even passive inhabitants of the space. And evidence abounds that those people trapped in food deserts without the kind of community activism to help provide and share fresh produce have increased consumption of processed foods and, in turn, are at higher risk of diabetes, cardiovascular disease, and obesity.[19]

The linkages that are potential here between food security, the environment, and health could not be more salient than now. Recently in the United Kingdom, but also in other countries around the world in the wake of the pandemic, governments have suggested that people take better care of themselves and manage their own health, particularly for minor issues, because post-pandemic hospital and GP queues and ambulance and junior doctors' and nurses' strikes have all put such burdens on our healthcare system that it is on the verge of being unable to treat let alone prevent serious illness. Pharmacies have been given greater scope and financial incentives to help answer queries and advise, to alleviate the financial pressures on crumbling health systems. While some pharmacists have cautioned that this places undue stress on their staff to advise in areas they consider complex or beyond the expertise of a pharmacist, the decentralised partnership that governments are encouraging people to have in managing their own health for minor problems is consistent with the kind of citizenship proposed in this book. What better time to imagine a community, when governments themselves are asking for it.[20]

Last winter, as the Jurassic clay soil in our small garden once again triumphed over the struggling few blades of grass that I so desperately hoped would pop up, persuaded by the projects of Tree and Cutteslowe and others, I declared to my children that I was rewilding the garden. Six months, half a pandemic, and two unprecedented droughts later, my children pointed out that my declaration basically amounted to letting the garden go to hell in a hand basket. Indeed, the few native 'ancient' grasses that I meticulously researched and bought online did not take. The blackberries and gooseberries of our home's previous owner burst through valiantly as my own attempts withered or, at best, grew modestly in a small and almost terrified way. The wild grasses that would have been native to this part of Oxfordshire near the meadow long ago will take time to grow and thrive; they will demand patience. But we need to go ahead and try. So grow your own tomatoes, spend time in that communal garden, grow as much of your own food as you reasonably can, responsibly, with species native to your land and using the principles that respect the environment. And then, most importantly, share your abundance, no matter its size, with others.

CHAPTER SIX

Eat 'Ethnic Food', Regularly

WHEN I BEGAN MY TEACHING CAREER IN THE Department of Government at Harvard University, I co-taught a graduate student seminar with the late Samuel P. Huntington, the formidable political scientist best known for his clash of civilisations thesis: the claim that future wars would be fought between cultures, not between countries. As we sat one humid afternoon in the poorly ventilated international affairs building, Sam presented some of his forthcoming work. It was perhaps his most controversial idea: he was suggesting both that American culture and American values were in decline, and that this was directly related to unprecedented Latino immigration. That is, of course, a condensed version of his more nuanced argument, but that afternoon, through the partially opened windows of that seminar room, salsa music from a car radio blared, drowning out his already fragile voice as he explained his thesis. For reasons only clear to me now, at that moment I had a sudden craving for the mouth-watering Mexican food my family and I often had when I was a child, served at holes-in-the-wall on the outskirts of Chicago. And I began to wonder whether we were all just enjoying too little so-called ethnic food for our own sense of not only tolerating but embracing our diversity. And that is to say: for our own good.

Race, ethnicity, religion, immigration, gender— diversity in all its permutations—are some of the most apparently stark lines along which we find or imagine our- selves to be divided, fighting for scarce resources. Living well in and with diversity is about one particular right— equality—and what the political theorist Michael Walzer has called 'toleration regimes', or the political arrange- ments for managing all this diversity and difference and trying to put into practice the idea that we are *all* equals.[1] This is and has always been a critically important, highly contested, and problematic theme of social life, across the world. It has always been with us, and has always been managed by the law. Certainly, many would agree that law has provided important blocks on unequal treatment, by opening marriage to non-heterosexual couples, reversing segregation, giving women the right to vote, decriminalising homosexuality . . . and the list goes on. But almost inarguably, if the law did ever help us here, help us to come together and enjoy our diversity, it was only after social movements pushed hard for change to undo previous laws that managed difference badly. Let's remember in this context Black Lives Matter, the anti-apartheid movement, #MeToo, and also the Monday demonstrations in Leipzig, the March on Washington, the women's suffrage movement, Occupy Wall Street, the Salt March, and so on. In many of these cases, rights to be tolerated and treated equally were literally extracted by people from the state, and, in many of these cases, problematic laws were changed to make way for these hard-won rights to equality.

And even then, we have to ask ourselves, has the existence of the new laws, for example those prohibiting discrimination, helped significantly, or have racism and homophobia and misogyny found other ways into our lives, into our systems? Take, for instance, the compelling research and arguments brought to us by civil rights litigator Michelle Alexander, who claimed that mass incarceration, as she defined it, basically amounts to a form of racialised social control that bears striking similarity to Jim Crow laws—to the laws mandating racial segregation.[2]

Has the law enabled us here with our diversity, or has it merely removed some blocks—and only in the best of cases? Despite ample laws, these themes—immigration, race, gender—are regularly listed among the top issues troubling our nations in public opinion polls. In 2022, for example, on social media alone, 'polling by Ipsos shows over four in five (84 per cent) adults in the United Kingdom are concerned about seeing harmful content—such as racism, misogyny, homophobia and content that encourages self-harm'.[3] Across Europe and Asia, across the Americas and Africa, we are all concerned about who gets included in the idea of 'us'. We worry about preventing divisive, harmful messages from getting to our kids. But I think that is not where to begin. The first step here is admitting that all our food is 'ethnic', or none of it is.

The rich cuisines to be found in each of our democracies are an important window into our cultural differences, into the very differences that are our reality. We can of course seek to ignore or deny the complexity of our communities and remain inside our own homes without ever venturing out. We can close ourselves off from the other. It would be easy to do because the rules we live by, the laws, have already done this; they have pasted over important differences in our communities in order to carve a single order. Just think about the slogans we hear all the time: one nation under God. British values. French *laïcité*. And so forth. If we continue to rely on the law to ask us for help here, for help understanding differences and embracing them, this is what we are likely to get: either the partition of our societies into what some elites believed were workable groups, separated between states as in India and Pakistan, or within, as in Belgium. Or the fantasy of a homogenous citizenry, like that of France or the United Kingdom.

The challenge is that many so-called nation-states, not just the United States but across the globe, were not simply built by such artificial legal arrangements but were first built by force so the laws could fit more evenly on top. Local cultures and local languages which existed for centuries were pushed into the home, away from public life, so state builders could construct states that had one official language and one cultural expression—the 'high culture', as it was called, a high culture that also informed and was born out of a higher law. State building, as we know from history, was and remains a bloody and con-tested process of homogenisation, from early modern France to Indonesia today. In such a regime, we couldn't really taste those excellent tacos because we wouldn't even know they existed. We may scarf Taco Bell's bean bur-ritos, the industrialised imitation, but only because they were a safe fantasy, a cowardly way of indulging our curi-osity and interest in our forbidden neighbour.

Ernest Gellner was one of the first political theorists to think about this and alert us to the problems of multi-ple nations living under one artificially carved state. One language, one school system, and—as Gellner put it—one high culture.[4] These were and are artificial constructs.

Indeed, many of the problems we have seen in almost all modern democracies, from the United States and Canada to Spain but also across Africa and the Middle East, involve tensions between subgroups, between peoples in the plural, peoples from different religions, cultures, and races, squeezed into a single sardine can, sealed with a single constitution.

Iraq provides a revealing example of the forced nation-state. Laws imposed by the British Mandate seemed to do nothing but fuel anger and resentment between groups that ever since have pulled the state apart at the seams. When I sat with Kurds and Iraqis at a round table in Baghdad in 2009, trying to help them design revenue-sharing rules that they could agree on, the legacy of their animosity was profound. Kurds insisted that they deserved a greater share of oil and gas than the rest of the country. Not only because it was located on their land. Not only because extracting it destroyed this land and would one day leave them with infertile soil. But because they saw it as a reparation, as payback for the repression they had experienced by others, including the British, being forced to live together under a single set of laws despite their clear and marked cultural and other differences.

The order created by state builders and solidified with a constitution appears stable, sure. It is stable on paper and in its adherence to the letter of the constitutional architecture of the state. But anyone whose family member has been blown up in separatist bombings in Belfast or

Madrid or Basra will tell you, this may generally be stable order, but it is not good. Laws that require people to get along, or even to live separately, will not work if we do not accept the idea of getting along, let alone embrace it.

One afternoon in 1996, I went to the newsstand near my tiny rental in Paris to get a copy of *Le Monde*, a daily paper traditionally published around lunchtime. The front page that day announced the death of my friend Carmen's father. Law professor Francisco Tomás y Valiente, who sat on Spain's Constitutional Court, had been assassinated by the armed Basque separatist organisation Euskadi Ta Askatasuna (ETA). Shot twice in the head during his office hours at the university where he taught for decades, Professor Tomás y Valiente had been an outspoken critic of the Spanish state's negotiation with terrorists. But, ironically, Tomás y Valiente was also a public intellectual who cautioned, through the media, that law means nothing without goodwill—and that goodwill, a necessity for making democracy work, was simply missing in Spain. A firm believer in the collective, he cautioned that the autonomous regions needed to proceed gradually with their autonomy, respecting the fact that the rest of Spain might not be ready to agree to the new arrangement, and that, at the same time, the rest of Spain needed to appreciate why their autonomy in critical areas was so deeply important to them. In short, he called for a mutual understanding, a goodwill on both sides. And despite their remarkable constitution, a document imitated and often considered for import around the world to multi-ethnic democracies, a document meant to appease tension and keep different nations together under one roof, he believed this goodwill was simply not yet there.

Partition laws, laws designed to help restore order in places where violent ethnic conflict erupted, work no better. For decades, partition advocates and theorists believed that separating groups into demographic enclaves—partitioning them—was the answer to stable law and order. But is that right? Nicholas Sambanis, director of the Identity and Conflict Lab at the University of Pennsylvania, spent a good part of his career trying to find out, using cutting-edge research methods and working with teams of scholars across countries. He found that, on average, 'partition does not significantly reduce the probability of new violence'.[5] Instead, he concluded, it is more important to establish what he called credible and equitable systems of government. Unfortunately, credibility and equality don't yet characterise most governments, let alone those in very divided states. Which brings us back to the groundwork we can and must do ourselves.

This particular form of civic virtue and goodwill towards the other, specifically towards someone who is a migrant, for example, and cooks rice a different way than I do, or who comes from the other side of the regional border and has a different native tongue from mine, has always been the most challenging hurdle for countries such as the United States, France, or the United Kingdom, where waves of immigration have brought a mosaic of peoples together in the same physical space. We find it hard to share, but we find it particularly hard to share with those who are visibly different from us—perhaps because we feel threatened that the 'others' will dilute our own culture, question our gods, take our territory, or simply change what we consider the basis of our identity. Often, this is based on long-standing myths that might be helpful for group cohesion but which provide an all-too-easy reason for exclusion. Where the law has been applied, it has mostly been used to set up separate spaces for different groups: through segregation; through federalism, which offers territorial separation of peoples; through legal exemptions from the law for particular groups that consider themselves simply too different from the rest, like the American Amish community. But no dividing line, no wall or boundary, no devolution of power will replace what is necessary: our mutual interest in those members of our larger community who are significantly different from us in some way or another.

Gender is part of this. And it adds yet another layer of complexity to race and ethnicity. The film *Thelma and Louise*, a story of two friends who flee to Mexico after one of them kills a man attempting to rape her, became a manifesto of sorts for many women of the 1990s, and others who felt frustrated by legal constraints, not because they wanted to break the law but because they wanted the law to protect them and found that, in large part because of who they were—women—the law often did not work for them. In writing about the film, former dean of Harvard Law School, Professor Martha Minow, and professor of philosophy Elizabeth V. Spelman, likened Thelma and Louise's frustrations to those of the non-white male, not to blur the important nuances and differences these men face but to illustrate some of the similarities. Because as they note 'the "noble" outlaw is an oddly revered character, loosely associated in United States folklore with the West and with romantic ideas about personal development and freedom. The paradigmatic noble outlaw is a male whose lawbreaking can be understood as in some sense virtuous.'[6] American culture does not allow us to imagine anyone other than a white man holding this esteemed position. The African American, the Mexican American, the Asian American, the woman—when they break the law to do something they consider virtuous, or right, they instead are viewed as not just 'deviant citizens' but deviants more generally. Problematic, not noble.[7] Our own folklore, our collective conscience, does not let us cross these dividing lines. It is the other—Black, white, brown, female, transgender—the other who is not like we are, however we define it, whom we need to accept and embrace, and yet it is the law that actually seems to fail these particular people more. Even very recently, experts in the United Kingdom interviewed more than three hundred legal professionals about bias in the judiciary. At the time of their interviews in 2022, 95 per cent said that racial bias plays a role in the processes or outcomes of the justice system, and 29 per cent said it played a 'fundamental role'.[8]

I do not think that by only eating more 'ethnic' food we are going to achieve toleration and civic virtue. It is symbolic, a bridge and a beginning to seeing the 'other' as interesting, and equal, to us. Food is something to be shared, and rich 'ethnic' cuisines are available to us, as part of who we are. And yet, while we might enjoy and eat the food of a different culture, we don't necessarily want to go further towards welcoming that culture into our lives or accepting it as part of who we are. So we need to start somewhere, and soon. Immigration is one of the most divisive issues for Americans now, with serious concerns about our borders, but it is also the case for Canadians, Italians, Germans, French—just about everywhere.[9] We are all worried about our security, about others arriving to our lands, and some are particularly worried about others 'diluting' our culture or taking local jobs and school places when we have worked so hard to get them ourselves.

Good food may be the cure—a different kind of chicken soup, for this very complex and hotly debated ailment. When I taught at Oxford, I required my first-year graduate students, in this ancient and still rather English university town, to venture a bit east and photograph a particular deli on Cowley Road. This road, with its twenty-mile-per-hour speed limit, is a bastion of ethnic and economic diversity, home to many, from wealthy All Souls dons to impoverished Syrian refugees. In the time it takes to walk the length of the road, you can find just about anything, from a halal butcher, to a mikveh, to a place to have your locs redone.[10]

My students would come back with a few photos, some excellent baklava, and lots of questions: questions mainly about themselves. About who they are and about what the United Kingdom is now. About how they relate to the other and to their research. About how to make sense of Brexit. And so on.

As a scholar whose work has taken me all over the world to critically engage in the laws and foundations of other places, I strongly believe that identities are best understood by tasting, viscerally experiencing, the other, and not just some mock fantasy version of them. It is a way of beginning to appreciate ourselves and our rich complexity. I am sure that Sam Huntington, the brilliant colleague from whom I learned so much, and who also appreciated good food and good culture, would have wholeheartedly agreed. It is perhaps no coincidence that when I left Iraq, the sheiks I worked closely with in their Committee on Constitutional Review and my Iraqi translator presented me with two very precious gifts: a box of local, fumigated dates and a bag of Basra limes. They were an invitation into their cultures, a breaking of bread across so many divides.

Such sharing does work. France, a former empire that extended from Africa to Asia to South America, welcomed a plethora of peoples of mixed races and cultures into its relatively tiny metropole. The mix has not always been peaceful. Indeed, some of the worst riots of the past decades have occurred in France, where peoples of colour felt let down by governments and integration projects failed, while poverty raged, and Islamic extremists tapped into discontent to fuel more violence and division. Even in what might be one of the most overdetermined cases of melting-pot failure in the developed world, there have been local successes.

In the mid-1990s, the suburbs a short train ride from the Eiffel Tower were described in the press as heartless and lacking community, places where just small groups of strangers with no connection to one another other than their despair would live out their days.

That was the way socialist historian Françoise Gaspard described Dreux, her hometown, where she was once mayor. Crime was rampant, and youths from North Africa were, rightly or wrongly, blamed for much of it. The National Front under Le Pen's leadership made massive gains among the older, white French Dreuxians, because it was one of the few political parties to directly engage with the question of race and immigration that was clearly an issue there.

Miro Rizvic managed a small shop in Dreux and struggled to maintain the business amid the petty crime that took profits away from his boss. But then, thinking through the problem one day, he found an innovative solution. 'I hire local people,' he said, 'a Moroccan for the vegetables, a Tunisian for the canned goods, a Turk for the cash register. That way they know just about everybody who comes in here. It's better than hiring security guards.'[11]

Rizvic, himself a recent French citizen, had emigrated some twenty years previously from Bosnia. Instinctively, perhaps, he understood what was necessary for cooperation across these ethnic divides.

Rizvic had found a form of good order that is the basis for cooperation in diverse communities around the world. Political scientists such as James Fearon and David Laitin spent their careers studying this kind of cooperation, and it is from them that I draw the Rizvic example. Working across potentially divisive lines is not only 'nice', it is critical to the functioning of the community, and to a thriving good order.[12]

It is also critical to development. Social scientists have long wondered why regions within a single country can vary so much in social and economic development. Countries such as Italy, but also India and Brazil, with their vast expanses of land in what we used to bizarrely refer to as the Third World, former colonies such as these, with embedded legacies of underdevelopment fed by both colonisers and foreign multinational corporations, have, in spite of many challenges, demonstrated remarkable pockets of 'good governance' in otherwise very complex and economically challenged national boundaries. But they were only pockets, and those studying them alerted us to the fact that the 'good governance' was mostly to do not with the governors at all but with the governed, with the qualities of the citizens themselves and their willingness to engage with the state and each other.

One of the first scholars to explore this regional variation in Brazil was the late Judith Tendler, an MIT economist.[13] More recently, Prerna Singh, a political scientist at Brown University, studied a similar pattern in India. Singh found that although illiteracy and poor health, malnutrition, and crime were rampant in many regions, there were these overachieving pockets in India in which citizens received better public goods, better schools and healthcare, enjoyed higher literacy rates, better and longer lives, and so forth. The key that Singh identified there was solidarity: a strong, shared sense of belonging to a community. This solidarity, this sense of each other and of their likeness, increased the chances that individuals in the community would work with regional elites to push for investment in the areas they believed were most necessary for taking care of the subunit, the community, and these tended to be health and education.[14]

So here is the question: How do we get that solidarity, that cooperation, even across different groups? Across ethnic and racial divides, across political lines? How do we get the young and old to sit down to a community project together and not bicker over which group is better able to advise and lead? How, then, to build solidarity? One answer might lie in the shells of hermit crabs.

There is a David Attenborough documentary which shows some funky-looking crabs crawling awkwardly across a seashore, looking almost hungover from a night out on the town. As they stumble and bump into one another, Attenborough explains that these hermit crabs are highly dependent on their shells for protection and that naked crabs are vulnerable to just about everything, from predators to sunshine. As they grow, their shells do not grow with them, so these crabs discard their old shells and need to find new ones to fit their more mature bodies. Like teenagers rapidly outgrowing their jeans, they jump at the chance to go shopping. Only in the crabs' case, the shopping spree is a matter of life and death. So what happens? Does this hermit crab shopping spree look something like the stampeding crowds we read about everywhere from Rio de Janeiro to Oakland, where shoppers turn up early for the holiday sales and wind up trampling staff and breaking hinges on doors to grab the bargains? Not at all. Instead, these animals usually organise themselves in the most interesting, cooperative way, in what some scholars have referred to as 'nature's housing market', apparently without the tricks and bribes and pathologies found in the human version of these market exchanges.

Biologist Mark Laidre in New Hampshire has studied these fascinating animals. He explains that the indispensable need these crabs have for shells sets up the potential for extreme conflict but actually results in elegant cooperation. What's even more interesting for us is that, unlike many forms of cooperation, it does not result from ties of kinship. Because of a 'planktonic dispersal stage' in the ocean, the crabs are separated from their kin before they reach land. That means they need to cooperate with non-kin—it's no longer the family that matters and helps you out. They do so by forming coalitions that help them find a well-fitting shell, sometimes evicting other crabs to get it, and the coalitions that tend to be the most stable are those in which smaller crabs and larger crabs work together.[15]

There is increasing interest in the ecology and evolution of these cooperative networks, especially those that go beyond kin, and evidence is emerging that ants and other creatures practise such cooperation outside of their families, sometimes outside of their own species. This is not the same as altruism, in which strangers come to the rescue of someone in need. Not all cooperation is selfless. It stems instead from the basic need we all share as living organisms, the need to survive. And when we realise that to meet this need we must cooperate with and take care of other living beings who are not necessarily members of our family, of our race, or even of our species, that's when a unique form of cooperation happens, the kind that, as scientists like Laidre say, is actually pretty robust and stable.

Of course, there is one reason for cooperating that is unique to humans, as far as we know, and not motivated simply by survival or our need to get something out of it. Very simply, you cooperate across lines because it is the right thing to do, the 'just' thing, the thing that contributes to and even maximises human dignity. This idea, that human dignity should be perhaps the most important motivating factor for us as we move through our lives, is so important that after World War II as I mentioned earlier, Germans carved it into their new foundation, their Basic Law. Having witnessed the complete disregard for human life during the Holocaust, legal framers made this the top value of their postwar political structure. Article 1, indeed sentence 1, of the German Basic Law reads, 'Human dignity shall be inviolable.' Of course, this is a law, even if it is higher law, and of all law I am sceptical. The key is not to see it carved into the law at all but, instead, to see it every day, not at a national level but in decentralised places, where individuals across different sides of some salient dividing line have come together to cooperate, not because of a natural disaster, not for mutual benefit, but, this time, because it was the right thing to do.

Like the feuding factions in Spike Lee's Brooklyn, there are examples of individuals who do actually do the right thing, simply for the sake of human dignity. Soldiers in the First and Second World Wars who did not shoot when ordered; Christian Germans and Dutch and French citizens who helped Jews by sheltering them, aiding their escape from the Nazis, risking their own lives repeatedly over an extended period of time. Russians who are standing up to their government, risking prison or death or worse, to denounce Putin and his war in Ukraine. Not for their own benefit but for their own humanity.

But we don't need things of great violence to see it. We can see the humanity of the individual before us, regardless of their gender, skin colour, sexual orientation. We can tolerate the things that are different if we realise that we are united in our humanity. We can then appreciate our differences, because we see that they, like 'ethnic food', actually make our community interesting. And so, we can do the right thing.

If as individuals we accept the dignity of all, how is it that we nevertheless get caught in our own homogenous enclaves? Without understanding why, when we are not opposed to diversity, we nevertheless seem to wind up in a place that is homogenous—and that is not prepared to do the right thing. The economist and Nobel laureate Thomas Schelling sought to understand this many decades ago; he wanted to know, for example, why people who don't identify themselves as racist nevertheless end up in segregated neighbourhoods. He studied individuals who expressed only slight resistance to being in a racially mixed neighbourhood, who were comfortable as long as they had one neighbour who looked like them; but he saw that often, these people still wound up with a collective outcome that was a strictly segregated neighbourhood.[16] Lamenting the fact that neighbourhoods often ended up so segregated through choice even though most people preferred some degree of integration, he set out to understand— using his strength, mathematical modelling—what could be done. His conclusion is not different from what most philosophers have called for over decades: increased toleration. Schelling referred to toleration schedules, or limits to how much one race (or gender or religious group) would tolerate the other group being present nearby. Increasing this limit, this toleration of the other, resulted in mixed neighbourhoods which were preferable to most. The mathematical dynamics of the collectivity mean that you have to increase your toleration enough to reach that threshold. Easier said than done. But it is another way of saying that we have to try even just a little bit more as individuals to understand and appreciate one another, so that together, as a collective, we get a much more inclusive neighbourhood.

Why can't we just let the law take care of all this? Well, for one, such laws will be contested by those who have the most to lose from them. And second, what we want is not only the outcome *but the process*. I know this sounds like the platitude about 'it's the journey that counts', but just look at the related issue of ending segregation in the United States. Many believed that landmark legal cases, such as *Brown v Board of Education*, helped end racial segregation in American schools and paved the way for further opportunities for citizens, regardless of the colour of their skin. But this is not necessarily the complete story. Even if we do believe that *Brown* was an important decision in favour of civil rights, that the law here worked, it didn't exactly help in the most positive, constructive way we think. Segregation was overruled, true, but enabling legislation that would actually help support people of different races to thrive in their educational settings didn't necessarily flow. Because even when the law works, it falls short. It removes blocks, perhaps, but does not necessarily provide incentives for the kind of engagement we want and need to move forward. That work is up to us.

In an important experiment devised by Jack Balkin at Yale Law School, several well-respected professors of constitutional law and legal theory were asked to rewrite opinions for *Brown* in a hypothetical exercise. The formidable scholar Catharine MacKinnon stated in her opinion that 'the risk we run today is not of going too far too fast, as defendants fear, but of going too slowly and not far enough'.[17] Waiting for the law to do our work is part of the entire problem, and, when it does change, it is slow, incremental, and not always in the direction we know is best for a cooperative solution to our problems.

But it is more than just rectifying the pace of legal compulsion. More convincing is the hypothetical dissenting opinion in this project presented by the equally formidable Derrick Bell, the first African American professor to be granted tenure at Harvard Law School: 'I dissent today from the majority's decision in these cases because the detestable segregation in the public schools that the majority finds unconstitutional is a manifestation of the evil of racism, the depths and pervasiveness of which this Court fails even to acknowledge, much less address and attempt to correct.' Indeed, he ends with, 'Negroes, who despite all are perhaps the nation's most faithful citizens, deserve better.'[18]

But even this, the law cannot correct. We must. And we can begin by sharing each other's 'ethnic food' regularly, real home-cooked food made by the many cultures that make up our communities. Go ahead and enjoy the diversity that we are, our human races, and maybe we might begin to really understand how we are different but also, how much we are the same.

CHAPTER SEVEN

Start This All Very
Early, About Age Three

A S A UNIVERSITY UNDERGRADUATE, I REMEMBER LEARN-
ing something about education, or the lack of it,
during a tense period of final exams. Fatigued by yet another
sleepless night of writing a one-draft wonder, desperate
after having just missed the 5 p.m. cut-off time for sub-
mission, finding a locked door at the faculty office, I came
up with a novel solution: the research paper home delivery.
Enlisting my enthusiastic friend Valery and her friend,

who owned a car, we popped into their manual-drive Ford Fiesta and headed a fair few blocks west to the calm Chicago suburb where my professor lived. While Valery and her friend crossed manicured lawns looking for the correct address, I lay down in back, ashamed to show the state of self-neglect I had indulged while finishing that work. But when after some time my friends hadn't returned, I popped my head up as if from a trench to see, in the early evening sky, a series of porch lights coming on like synchronised fireflies. Porch after porch, people were lighting up, watching this not-so-interesting home term paper delivery. What—why? Because this was a white, middle-class, and apparently educated neighbourhood. It was early evening. And my friends were Black.

If the law is not necessarily encouraging us to respect one another and celebrate our differences, if it is not sufficient to prevent such a scene, we have to ask what will. And so the search for a real citizenry ends where it should begin: with education. A real one.

Jean-Jacques Rousseau is known for his work on the social contract, the agreement we would all make with each other in establishing an authority to govern us. Talk of the broken social contract has been everywhere of late, with some of our most important intellectuals pointing out that many peoples were not included in those social contracts to begin with.[1] Now scholars and pundits are offering ways to fix it. But this is not the Rousseau we should be looking for now. Rousseau's lesser-known work was on children—and it is critical to understanding how he envisioned a social contract working in the first place, for he warned against a form of education that relied on institutions and rules, and instead he believed that education should be about learning to think for yourself and about others. And the key to achieving that, for him, rests on solidarity and empathy. In fact, education was so important to his social contract theory that he suggested the contract could only really work if we made the right contract with our kids first.

Whether you have an average child, a gifted child, a special needs child, data is showing us that our current education systems are failing our children, leaving them behind in basic life skills, such as reading and writing, and under-stimulating their minds.[2] Perhaps part of the problem is that we remain very Victorian, for many of these institutions are still based and focused on authority and hierarchy and, either directly or through outdated and biased curricula, on exclusion, when they need to begin with the child: the self-organising child, who knows instinctively what they want to learn. This child needs, as Maria Montessori said, a guide rather than an authority figure, to help them negotiate their learning and their responsibility as a citizen in an increasingly diverse community.

Here's what I mean.

In the small town of Reggio Emilia in northern Italy, an experiment with early childhood education, one that had roots in Rousseau's theories, exploded into a global phenomenon. Every year, teachers travel from all over the world to study the 'Reggio Emilia' preschools. These preschools were initiated by parents after the Second World War, projects that resulted from partnerships between these parents and the city council. They are now need-based municipality-run schools that fund them-selves through progressive taxes and progressive contribu-tions from families. And they are so unique that, in 1991, *Newsweek* rated them among the Ten Best Schools in the World. Yes, preschools.

When you walk into any of these preschools of Reg-gio Emilia, you notice several things that are deliberately different from the preschools of other countries, or even the preschools in other parts of Italy. First, and most importantly, you notice the location of a large and invit-ing common space where children are meant to wander and congregate and interact throughout the school day. It is called, fittingly, the piazza. The preschools in Reggio Emilia have embodied this concept, the idea of the piazza and its role in encouraging us to meet, deliberately pro-voking this spontaneous interaction among the children in the school. As a teacher in one of the schools told me, 'We are forming citizens and building community, we are not a parking lot for children while their parents work.'

When my son was three and offered a place at one of these schools, we went to meet with his class teacher. A Beaux-Arts-trained atelierista greeted us at the door, and as we walked through the vast open space, we noticed children emerging from the piazza. A young boy in high-heeled shoes and a feather boa stumbled forward to inspect my son, his new colleague. Smiling, he and his dress-up playmate greeted us and then continued their important creative work as we toured the school. I compare this memory in my mind to my daughter's former preschool in Oxford, an award-winning architectural building and Oxford college nursery, which in spite of its amazing construction lacks a piazza. You enter a small space, which diverts you around a corner. Areas are divided up by activity. It is a lovely structure, with incredible natural materials. But the idea of a welcoming, open space for children and parents to mix and congregate and engage—is absent. Without it, common knowledge, the critical basis for cooperation, is absent, too.

Culturally, some countries and societies are better at doing this, at creating the proper public spaces for common knowledge. And in Reggio Emilia, Italy, it is so important, so critical to how the Italians have always thought about their spaces, that they start their kids off with it at age three. There are, of course, other pedagogical examples from other countries. But what is striking and apparently unique about Reggio Emilia is that these schools are rooted in a culture that, at least for a while, and centuries ago, believed in thinking about the 'other' and encouraged civic virtue. Although a country whose traffic laws are often considered suggestions rather than firm rules, it is also the country whose people were the first in

Europe to suffer the devastation of COVID-19 but came together quickly and embraced self-isolation with humour and solidarity. Perhaps it is the experience with both aspects of Italian culture that leaves the countless teachers who come from all over the world to take workshops on the Reggio Emilia Approach inspired but also realistic.

The road for those of us whose cultures are rooted not in community and friendship but in *individual liberty* will be long. But we must begin somewhere. If we can achieve the development of our personalities so that we are, following Cicero and early Roman law, civic-minded individuals, we free ourselves from the constraints of laws and rules not to fall into complete disorder but to let a good social understanding emerge so that the laws and rules have less work to do. We must stop worrying about whether Chinese children are outperforming the Germans in information and communication technology and instead help our children, first and foremost, to internalise their sense of belonging to humankind and acting like it. Especially in the early years.

Education will always be difficult to reform, for it is run by government, with our tax money, and is a critical element of the modern state, even those in Reggio Emilia, which are local initiatives and run in partnership with the state. These are not fancy, posh private schools. They are fancy, posh state schools—where fancy refers to the sophisticated understanding of pedagogy and child development brought to bear on the work done by teachers in

the school, and posh refers to the rich variety of materials and projects available to all children. In bringing the
local government and local citizens' community together
at a small round table to think about what they wanted
to provide for the young citizens of Reggio, a pedagogical
phenomenon was born.

Outside of Sudbury, Massachusetts, sits the home of
another model, the Sudbury Valley School. Here students as young as five and as old as seventeen sit together
as equals with staff, for there is no hierarchy, and no one
plays follow the leader. Founded in 1968 as a form of education based on direct democracy, there are now dozens
of these schools throughout the world. I had a video chat
during the pandemic with one graduate of such a school in
the United States who went on to college and now works
with computers. I wondered whether such a protective,
and different, educational environment, such as the Sudbury model, had made it more difficult for him to enter
the 'real' world.

'A great question,' he responded, confidently and eloquently. 'I can see how it might. But I actually felt like
I had an advantage.' He went on to tell me that after his
Sudbury education, while in college, he had absolutely no
problem asking his roommates and classmates for help
when he needed it. When he didn't understand something, he didn't feel ashamed or feel a desire to fake it. He
didn't feel the sort of competition that many of us grew up
with, in which you know that if you are being graded on a

curve, helping your classmate does not necessarily help you get a better mark and so becomes irrational. Rather, this young man said he knew intuitively what to do: where to look things up, how to teach himself, and how to simply ask his peers for help and advice, without having to appeal to an authority figure at all. This is the purpose of such education: to instil in young citizens, whom we tend to overlook or fail to see as citizens, the trust and belief in their own capacity, their own capabilities, and, from there, the mutual trust and respect of their peers.

I visited a small libertarian school just outside of Verona, on a hillside that overlooks stepped countryside and is bathed in sunshine all day. This experiment similarly attempts to build a community through democratic management: all kids have a vote on the agenda, decisions are taken together through compromise. It is more difficult to run a school this way, it takes longer to get things done. It is disorderly, but that disorder is an investment. I toured the space with my young children as the school coordinator and guide led us around. As lunch was approaching, my son became impatient, and his blood sugar began to drop. Our guide, without hesitating, asked the small group of students who had brought their lunch boxes whether each would be willing to give a tiny bit of their lunch, small donations that would together make a whole portion for my son. Small donations, big gestures. This is one of the many lessons of the day in that school, delivered spontaneously and concretely, not on a whiteboard at the front of the room. Not unlike the human-scale, collective outcomes education movements which attempt to reduce class and school sizes, these projects seek to understand first our relationship to each other and to the space around us, and our responsibility for fostering those relationships. This becomes the basis for building knowledge and the basis for future generations of citizens who have that sense of relationships in their moral fibre, who do not have to learn these things for the first time when they are adults. Rather, they internalise it early, across social and racial lines, and they practise it often.

This type of education, and this type only, underscores our civil obedience to ourselves and each other, and prevents any spontaneous project from developing into the kind of hierarchical, mind-control groups so reminiscent of the 1970s. We are not creating obedient, authoritarian cults; we are rebuilding humanity from the bottom up, one thoughtful child at a time.

This is not to ignore the fact that we want children to learn to read and write, to know facts about the world, and to be exposed to all the fascinating subjects out there, from geography to art to physics and music. As James Handscome, executive principal of Harris Westminster Sixth Form, a selective secondary school accepting students from areas of socioeconomic deprivation in London, rightly pointed out to me, qualifications are important, and disadvantaged students are those most likely not to have qualifications or maybe not to have developed a love of learning. 'We have to think carefully about how we're providing for those who find study difficult, what we're doing to enrich their lives, to improve their confidence, to set them up for the future.'[3] Indeed, and that is why we must plant the seeds of community, empathy, and connection earlier—in preschools and primary schools, so that secondary schools can then build on this foundation but concentrate on educating students in the subjects they will need to survive and thrive in our increasingly complex world.

So, will this be costly? Not financially, for the Reggio Emilia schools had early roots in the late 1860s, in the small village of Villa Guida, where people lived in poverty. Wanting to give children a physical and moral space within which to grow and understand community, they were some of the first attempts at a secular citizen education. As Fascism took hold in Italy, these schools were closed until after the war, when a group of parents began resurrecting the idea of a secular moral space and began building a preschool, physically, with bricks and mortar and their own labour, for the local children.[4]

Reggio stands out and has proven itself as a sustainable model, because it is one of the few projects that is inclusive of all, in that its funding by the local government and sliding scale of donations makes it affordable for all families. Moreover, in linking with the community in multiple ways, Reggio makes its project both more durable and more sustainable with backward and forward linkages. On a side street in central Reggio Emilia, not far from the many artisan gelaterias that also make this town special, is REMIDA, a joint project of the Reggio commune and Enia, a utility company.

REMIDA collects, cleans, and organises discarded products donated by about two hundred manufacturers throughout the region. Teachers from the Reggio schools then visit the centre daily to choose from remarkable materials for the children to use in their projects. Loose parts. From fabrics to paints, metals to plastics, paper and pieces of electrical wire, rubber, and so forth, these children benefit from the vast and diverse set of materials available to them at virtually no cost to the school. Rooted in British painter and sculptor Simon Nicholson's theory from the 1970s but brought up to date by establishing a no-waste loop via REMIDA, this initiative offers an endless number of configurations that come from the assembly of these raw materials. Play and learning become processes without end, not goalposts based on national curricula. The children create their world, impart their meaning, and in so doing are empowered because they are not simply presented with something and taught how to use it; they are given bits of nothing and encouraged to find something there. And they do. So, from age three, these children are solving problems their own way, with their own imaginations. What terrific preparation for a future which will demand of them equal creativity to solve real problems— from saving the environment to challenges posed by the exploration of space to the new and deadly viruses and bacteria that will inevitably arise.

Equally important is the knowledge these children and their parents and the community have that they are reusing things, that they are creatively turning discarded materials into beautiful works of art, that they are contributing to the sustainability of our world. In their own words, 'REMIDA is a cultural project of sustainability, creativity and research on waste materials. It promotes the idea that waste, the imperfect, is the bearer of an ethical message, capable of soliciting reflection, proposing itself as an educational resource, thus escaping the definition of being useless and rejected.'[5]

What we need to think about, then, is a form of early education that begins with these ideals and values: the community, the identities of the people in that community however complex it may be, sustainability and creativity, and the celebration of the imperfect. And that leads to the next important part of education.

Back in the 1980s, three adolescent boys in Norway committed suicide in what was widely believed to be a consequence of severe bullying by their peers. Norway's Ministry of Education reacted by initiating a campaign against bullying. Dan Olweus, a professor of psychology at the University of Bergen, firmly believed that bullying was a human rights problem, and, inspired by the fate of these boys and others, he carved one of the most effective strategies for the prevention of bullying that ever existed and which has been used, evaluated, and replicated in schools across the world for some thirty-five years. Olweus's tried and tested method has four basic principles which, when implemented, dramatically reduce the culture of bullying in the setting.[6]

The first principle requires adults in the school to be warm and show a positive interest in the kids, to actually be involved, to smile at them genuinely, to pat them on the shoulder and praise them—all kids, not just a few of them—in order to build a sense of trust with the group. The second principle requires setting boundaries, making clear what is an acceptable behaviour and what is not. The third implements consistent, non-hostile and nonphysical consequences for transgressions. And the fourth principle requires adults to function as positive role models—they must not be bullies themselves. They are principles based on values that we need to inculcate now in schools so that later, in our communities, we don't have bullies—we have cooperative, empathetic citizens.

What is striking about this programme is that, while it relies on structures of authority in the school and classroom to work, it seems aimed at trying to correct what authority has unfortunately become in institutions including schools: negative, disinterested, sometimes violent and aggressive, either actively or passively, often self-interested, and always controlling. What is fascinating here is that the main principles of this overwhelmingly effective anti-bullying programme focus in the first instance not on the kids but on the adults—on how we are leading and teaching our future generations, through the behaviours and attitudes we show them every single day. And when other kids are brought into the programme, it is in a way that encourages them to be responsible and active bystanders. 'Praise bystanders with specific comments about things they did to help, even if they were not effective,' Olweus's guide has it.[7] This is what we need to begin if we want to avoid letting our kids grow up to be the guilty bystanders described earlier.

Another educational pioneer who is often quoted in alternative pedagogical circles is Vasily Sukhomlinsky, a Ukrainian teacher who focused on the moral development of the child, rather than education for utilitarian purposes. Common to the theories of Sukhomlinsky, or the father of the Reggio approach, Malaguzzi, and many alternative educators, common to the local projects that worked, including Reggio Emilia but also Maria Montessori's school in Rome and Sukhomlinsky's village school in Ukraine, are three ideas we can easily replicate and tailor to our particular cultural needs:

1. Educate the very young to be kind and thoughtful citizens, not test takers.
2. Include and engage all.
3. Build backward and forward linkages between kids and the community, including the earth.

Obviously, their theories are richer and more nuanced than these three principles. But if you imagine most educational establishments in the world, it is striking how few combine these ideas. Vea Vecchi is an artist who worked as one of the first atelieristas in the Diana preschool in Reggio Emilia. When I attended a workshop at the Malaguzzi Centre one sultry Italian spring, I listened to Vecchi give a lecture. An elegant and graceful woman, she had spent more than thirty years at the preschool while also maintaining her own art practice. Vecchi has said in several places that throughout the decades, Reggio pedagogy has been 'built up in the daily work of many women and cared for by female minds and hands'.[8] Vecchi went on to claim that although she lamented the clear deficiency of male counterparts in the more recent history of the Reggio schools, what has nevertheless emerged in Reggio over the years of mainly female custodianship is a 'female' pedagogy, 'an education based on the values of relations, empathy, solidarity, of caring for things, tenderness and grace; all traits that psychology has traditionally attributed to the female gender, but that constitute richness for everyone'.[9]

I was struck by several of her suggestions and could not help thinking about another woman of similar age and physical stature, some three thousand miles away, with a different background and profession but who is perhaps united with Vecchi by her belief in, among other things, a 'female' philosophy. In a video I show my students, the legal philosopher Martha Nussbaum, walking along the shores of Lake Michigan near the University of Chicago, talks about something very similar: the importance of reimagining the public sphere and civil society more generally, not in the tradition of Hobbes and John Locke and most of our founding philosophers, all able white males, but something else, as a place of difference, where bodies and minds are not equal, where some are strong and others weak, and where the ideal role of the state might just actually be that of a nanny: to care for and educate, to nourish and include and entertain, particularly the most vulnerable.[10] Now a nanny state is often seen pejoratively, as one that cares whether its citizens wear seatbelts, eat too much sugar, smoke, drink, eat artery-clogging food, engage in debasing behaviour, and so forth—and so that state legislates accordingly, and with equal resistance. But let's instead imagine a nanny citizenry that works according to the female minds and hands of Reggio Emilia, one that, like the preschools, serves not to control and confine in the iron cage; a 'state' that we build together to help empower and encourage solidarity, empathy, grace, and tenderness.

But a child's piazza, of course, is not found only in the school nor is their education. To build future citizens, we need to build and reconceive playgrounds. And access to these playgrounds must be structured into the school day so that kids have time to be there.

It isn't only a question of time, however. The Austrian government has data suggesting that 70 per cent of girls they interviewed said they feel intimidated to join play-ground activities where boys are present.[11] What we don't even think about is how all our public piazzas, including children's play piazzas, are gendered and perhaps even prohibitive to those of colour, those on the spectrum—basically to many of our children who might not be exactly right down that elusive 'middle'. What would a gender-neutral, colour-blind, and disability-friendly play space look like? And how can we invite local governments into a dialogue with us, with our children, about what we want and what we need?

Such a vision may seem an incredible opportunity for a landscape architect, a city council, a group of citizens, to think through collectively and put it into practice. In the 1930s, Denmark did just this. It was witnessing, as was Germany and most of Europe, the emergence of fascism. At least one landscape architect in that inter-war Danish scene began thinking of ways to encourage a liberal, social attitude in the population to counter the coming anti-democratic one, an attitude that could bring families together in public spaces, allowing those in cities to enjoy the green spaces he thought necessary for health and wellbeing—but also bringing together the liberally minded community, trying to encourage it and help it thrive. Such spaces existed to some extent in the countryside, but the economic climate of the 1930s meant city dwellers had less access. Carl Theodor Sørensen thought this so important that he proposed city spaces that would begin with young children and allow them a place to engage with each other and with nature, a space that took gender and variations in abilities and ages into account but that did so in a way that encouraged growth and empowered the kids. Cottage Park was one such proposal, and it chimed with some of the more progressive voices in Europe at the time, from those who were fighting the rising tide of illiberal thought, including Alva Myrdal, the Swedish sociologist and Nobel laureate who lamented that preschools in her native land effectively divided children rather than bringing them together: poor families with working mothers were provided, at best, with basic care facilities which lacked any pedagogical innovation or stimulation; wealthy families could provide private governesses or more sophisticated, personalised, and sometimes overwhelming and rigid schools. Two extremes. Arguing the importance of closing the gap and doing so in the middle, with a better project for all, Myrdal and others theorised physical spaces and forms of early education that would help form citizens and perhaps even keep the emerging fascists at bay.[12] These early ideas share much with the philosophy behind Montessori's pedagogy and the pedagogy underpinning the Reggio Emilia schools. But they also speak to the spaces beyond the preschools, outside of them, the public spaces for all.

With the arrival of full-blown war in the 1940s, many such projects were put on hold. But the immediate postwar period and the defeat of the Nazis in Europe provided a second chance. Observing children playing amid the rubble of a Danish Second World War bomb site, Sørensen was apparently struck by the fact that children of various ages were moving carefully through this site, finding opportunities to play, to build familiar 'objects' such as dens and cars from the brick and mortar pieces lying at their feet. This ignited an idea for a new type of playground—no longer overly designed and architecturally complete but instead deliberately incomplete, a work in progress that he said would resemble 'junk' to the adult eye but provide endless opportunity for creativity and cooperative play in the child's eye. The 'junk' playground was born. Sørensen went on to help found the first of these playgrounds, the now-famous Emdrup Junk Playground in Copenhagen, which has been frequently cited as the birthplace of playwork. Sørensen is said to have commented that in his career, architecturally, the junk playground was by far his ugliest idea but also his most significant and the one of which he was most proud.[13]

Across the North Sea, and around the same time, an English landscape architect, the Lady Allen of Hurtwood, became a major force advocating for these junk playgrounds in the United Kingdom after the war. These are not the playgrounds built by anyone else, the steel and wood structures with a corporate logo on their underframe. Rather, they are made of random pieces of discarded material, some donated, some found, where the adventure is imagined by the children themselves, created in their minds and collaboratively. In fact, they were sometimes referred to as adventure playgrounds for this reason.

If you entered Koop Adventure Playground in the United States on 15 October 2021, you would have seen kids outside with masks creating a COVID vaccine from mud and water for the under-twelve age group, their own idea, as scientists and governments debated and argued and then rushed to do the same. But these kids acted. A job advertisement for a playworker at Koop explains the role of an adult in this space, making it clear to applicants that 'sometimes our quiet presence, willingness to engage in un-adulty things and our practiced active listening leads to personal and therapeutic conversations with children about their lives and their struggles. Even if it just looks like playing in the mud or slaying zombies.'[14] Adventure play, risky play, junk playgrounds, and the idea of listening to the space that is not yet created but which is together imagined, all in the name of allowing young citizens to think about what they need and then create a version of it in a safe place.

The idea behind many of these junk playgrounds remains the same: creativity, playwork, community, cooperation, and resilience. These are things we have already been talking about building in this book, but the key is really starting kids out with them, giving them this foundation as they navigate their lives. Uniting all of these concepts, which also happen to be in the taglines of endless podcasts and bestselling parenting books, is the idea of risk—of allowing, and even encouraging, children to take risks that will teach them autonomy and resilience but also teach them community: how to rely on and help others. Any adult watching these children in a junk playground or its equivalent sees them climb the high trees or use real tools or light fires and will, invariably, at some point, cringe with an instinctual fear. For these children are indeed taking risks, but in so doing, and in a space where adults have minimised hazards, they are developing a sense of themselves, of their possibilities and their limits, and also a sense of each other. Because risk, the experts explain, is not the hazards in themselves, absolutely understood. Risk, rather, is a calculation, a judgement as to when a potential hazard is likely to cause harm and when it is not. Risky play is now well understood in the literature on child development as a healthy, even necessary, element in physical, cognitive, and emotional development. A systematic review of research studies on risky play 'revealed overall positive effects of risky outdoor play on a variety of health indicators and behaviours, most commonly physical activity, but also social health and behaviours, injuries, and aggression'.[15] These are all crucial for getting that solidarity and empathy that build community.

I end with the Land, another junk playground, made internationally popular by a documentary film that showed young children climbing tall trees with weak branches, while adult 'facilitators' watched (anxiously but patiently) below, stemming their natural instinct to tell a child to come down or be careful. In one scene, a girl of about ten years burns her finger on a large fire. The film is reminiscent of another made in London quite a few decades ago, showing children engaged and happy and moving curiously through a makeshift space of their own design and creation in the middle of a grim UK winter. Looking at these spaces as an adult, one recoils: they are really full of ugly junk, of old cardboard boxes and broken planks of wood, of discarded plastic crates and shapeless, unrecognisable things. And there is, in most of these spaces, a randomness: no orderly climbing frames or slides, no AstroTurf or rubberised bark, no corporate playground design that has thought through the placement of objects using calculations of distance between activities and expected number of participants and so forth. Rather, these spaces look like the dilapidated bomb sites they grew out of. They are messy, covered in dirty, broken—and here is the key— loose pieces. For the theory of loose parts is at the heart of learning here. To the child's creative eye, this is not a mess to be cleared and recycled; it is all the realm of possibility. No adult can intervene and restrict play and creativity in the name of order or cleanliness. No parent can complain that it is chaotic or that objects are improperly used. This space is sovereign in its mess and disorder, and so are the children who create within it. They do not need to worry about parents telling them not to break things. Not to get things dirty. They also do not have the false sense of security that comes with built-up playground spaces, which research has shown can actually be dangerous precisely for this reason.

In 2016, researchers from various disciplines at the University of Gloucestershire set out to understand whether these junk playgrounds of decades ago actually had any good effects, to find out whether the kids involved with them around Bristol and Gloucester for the past decades could show that they made some positive difference. Interviewing anyone, from the adults who visited the playgrounds as children to the now elderly parents or playworkers who observed and facilitated them, the researchers set out to gather information and produce a timeline trajectory that looked not only at the ups and downs of the development, use, legal restrictions, and funding issues concerning these playgrounds but also at the impact these spaces, *these piazzas*, had on young citizens as they grew. One conclusion the researchers came to was that the data that does exist, which is nevertheless patchy, 'tends to show the instrumental value of adventure playgrounds and playwork in terms of its capacity to address social policy concerns such as reducing physical inactivity and obesity, crime reduction, or community cohesion'.[16]

We have evidence that the appropriate educational settings can be created, architecturally and substantively, to encourage an inclusive, bottom-up rights negotiation from an early age, by making use of the piazza both concretely and metaphorically, by engaging young people early on in forms of risky play and social stories that allow them to learn to work horizontally and cooperatively without excessive leadership. And by introducing innovations I've discussed in these examples, ones based on empirical research and grounded in a desire to bring us closer together—we begin to bring the pillars in this book together and plant seeds for future citizens.

So it all comes together here, with our very young kids, our very young citizens. Helping them learn not to play follow the leader, to own their rights, but responsibly, in a bottom-up rights negotiation, to hang out repeatedly in their piazzas, their play spaces, and to feel welcome there, to grow their own food and share it with others, to also eat so-called ethnic food and see it as part of their own mosaic identity.

Schools have to adopt all of these pillars in micro format and embed them in the curriculum as a priority. Call it 'deep' education.[17] We now know that our brains are much more plastic than we had originally thought, even adult brains, and that solidarity in the form of compassion and even altruistic behaviour can not only be encouraged; it can actually be taught.[18] But it is best to begin encouraging this altruistic, cooperative behaviour early. Evidence that it works already exists from researchers at the University of Wisconsin–Madison who set out to understand whether altruistic, cooperative behaviour could be learned by humans. Their research was so overwhelmingly positive that they developed the Kindness Curriculum, a programme that helps preschoolers learn how to take care of others, how to feel what others feel. Through a series of guided meditations that put kids in touch with their own feelings first, both emotional and physical, and then help them imagine how these feelings exist in others, they actually taught empathy—not what it is but how to have it. According to Professor Richard Davidson and his colleagues at UW-Madison, the idea of a 'connection'—a subjective sense of care and kinship for other people and not just one's relatives—can be promoted. In fact, his research was so compelling that he founded the Center for Healthy Minds, which supports schools across the country who are trying to use these techniques to build connection between our future citizens.[19]

Let's do this and start it with a curriculum for citizens, one that begins with empathy and moves on from there to solidarity, forming responsible, civic-minded citizens from about age three.

Conclusion

IF MY MESSAGE IS SO IMPORTANT, SO VITAL TO OUR world as I make it seem, why has what I propose not yet been done? Why is it necessary now? The past few years alone have shown us why, for we have lived through what may ultimately prove the most cataclysmic period—2020–2022—of the century, in which governments failed us and we, instead of them, acted. Lagos, BLM organising, mutual aid societies, and other examples I've explored in these pages are important beginnings, and they are real. The key now is to understand that they should not be exceptional paths, exceptional movements in the face of brutality or disasters, but rather, they should be part of our everyday approach to life. And the seedlings for this approach are there, in our present day and our histories.

The forest fires of the American Southwest are often unstoppable and their destruction complete. They were one July as I flew over the hills of northern New Mexico, on my way to the Santa Fe Institute, a place that would ignite my imagination and plant some of the seeds for this book.

Arriving at the airport, I briefly wondered whether I needed to change currency. I had only flown over from Boston, but it seemed another world. Outside, low adobe buildings punctuated dry earth. I landed now not in the hell of a war zone but in a sandcastle in the middle of the desert.

As I drove to the SFI, I looked out at the foreign land and remembered Amy, a Harvard student, a young woman of Navajo ancestry. Somewhere out there, I thought, was her home. And I recalled a moment in our seminar when someone referred to her as a Native American. 'Well,' she said, matter-of-factly, 'I'm an Indian. For us, if you would call yourself a Native American, you would just sound like an asshole.'

Identities—the ways in which people perceive themselves and others—are here and everywhere multiple and contested. Battlefields still exist, but they are intangible and internal. The sand is all silent but continues to tell very complex tales. In New Mexico it certainly does, but also in Chicago and New Orleans. And Tel Aviv, Jaipur, and Lima.

Conclusion

Identities are, perhaps, the most challenging part of civility, of being a citizen. I don't pretend for a moment that what I am calling for here in these pages, our work together, will be easy. To come together spontaneously and help one another, we must first have a sense of ourselves, and few of us actually do.

I know that the projects mentioned in this book, and my six ideas for making democracy work now, may seem exceptional and utopian, costly and risky, or, worse, insignificant. But in believing this, dismissing out of hand any ideas such as mine as too radical, utopian, or inadequate, we run an even greater risk—the risk of missing critical experiments that could bring long-needed change. We can continue to complain, or we can begin to take necessary risks ourselves. It is time we stop the endless protest culture, the blocking of government using violence and disruption when we are dissatisfied with policy and the state. There may have been a time in history for civil disobedience, to be sure. But the time has come for civil obedience—not to an authority or state but to ourselves.

Research across the social sciences that I engaged with in these chapters has shown that there are two basic elements that are necessary for communities to thrive and survive, even in the face of crisis, and even without governments: resilience and adaptation. These are what we need to fortify now and to nourish. We need to encourage our capacity, as individuals, to come together spontaneously in communities that are resilient and adaptable.

Through the six steps, the six pillars of citizenship I have outlined here, I believe we can make a good start.

It will be hard. But it has never been more necessary. Over the past few years, we have lost our sense of self, our sense of community, with twin processes that saw our public spaces close because of the pandemic and our phones and computers overload with global 'information'. Our loyalties to small, local groups, once critical to our identities, are in flux. While this might have the positive effect of nudging us out of parochial enclaves, it also means we are more challenged to define ourselves and to know where we feel comfortable because we actually feel comfortable, not because some algorithm tells us we do. We have been shaken by the failures of governments, no doubt, but also by the failures of some of our most visible social groups, with sexual abuse scandals rocking entities as diverse as the Catholic Church, Hollywood, and USA Gymnastics. Our trust in our groups, our own communities, has plummeted.

Disasters have also tested our commitment to our communities, from the earthquakes in Haiti and Japan to the forest fires in California. From gun violence in Orlando and pretty much everywhere else in the United States to terrorist attacks in Paris and London and Boston, in order to survive we have been forced to run away from each other and to think mostly of ourselves. The crises will continue, there will be more. But this is not the entire story, nor should it be. We have also shown incredible commitment to the human race in these dark times.

One of the best explanations for change—how fundamental change happens—came from one who should certainly understand it: virologist and creator of the polio vaccine Jonas Salk used the simple schematic of the sigmoid curve to illustrate how he believed populations changed. If we imagine an elongated S shape, in which the beginning of change is slow and flat like the bottom of the S, and the end of change is also slow and flat like the top of the S; but the middle, that crucial middle, in which the letter swings upward and over to a different curve, that is the crucial part of change: it is here, at the inflection point, that change happens; it happens steeply and rapidly, and it is also here, then, that resistance to change is strongest.[1] And here we find ourselves.

Another letter schematic can also help us understand. Imagine now an elongated letter J, with its slow dip before the long climb upward. Scientists have long used the J-curve to explain all sorts of change, from the efficacy of medical treatments to economic growth to international trade. But one of the most interesting uses of the J-curve to illuminate social change was published by my former fellow graduate school classmate, Joel Hellman, in the late 1990s.[2] Witnessing the painful experiences of simultaneous economic and political reform in the post-communist countries after the fall of the Berlin Wall, Hellman wanted to examine why so many of them saw their reforms stall midway. Citing the J-curve, he explained that most analytical work documented relative deprivation as the cause.

That means that people suffering from the governmental austerity programmes, the sudden and rapid privatisations of state industry, and other reforms deemed necessary to create a market economy, would see a short-term, painful, and quite negative impact on their lives before improvements came, before they could reap any benefits. These people, scholars believed, would get so fed up that they would block the reforms from going further, and the rewards would never come. It was a plausible theory, but what Joel ingeniously uncovered in his research was that it was not the short-term losers suffering at the bottom of that J-curve who blocked further reforms before they had a chance to get better and shoot up. Rather, Joel discovered that it was the short-term winners, those profiting from private rents and early distortions in the period of rapid change, the few who reaped benefits from the hardship of others, stopping things. The challenge, he concluded, was not so much to marginalise the losers and insulate governments from their protests but to include the losers and control those short-term, greedy winners.

There is no doubt in my mind that any and all of the changes that I am suggesting in this book will lead to plenty of J-curves, sigmoid curves, distortions and disruptions and greedy short-term winners and so forth—*at least* in the short term. Change brings resistance, not only from those who stand to lose but also from those who gain early. The only solution, therefore, is to allow this change to happen not as a top-down elite strategy but as a cooperative, community-based agreement from the bottom, one that includes short-term losers and winners and brings them through the process together to complete the curve, so that all are able to reap the benefits when they do eventually come.

To do this, we need to embrace the useful disorder of human nature and its power to regenerate itself, by itself. Nature, left to its own devices and with the right conditions, the right incentives, will find order. This nature can be ecosystems, bubbles in a petri dish, and even people in a community. When external actors such as governments come along and think they are helping by putting rules, laws, and constitutions in place, they often mess it up, for they have always tried to provide order through stability and control, instead of through incentives for learning and spontaneous cooperation. Now more than ever is our chance to create and build this good, true order—one that is dynamic and responsive, one that emerges spontaneously, one that is never, ever static.

How to Be a Citizen should not be confused with a call for either unqualified neoliberalism or anarchy, though the reader might find similarities insofar as the very best and fairest experiments within these ideologies rely on spontaneous order. What I envision is definitely not to be confused with the storming of government buildings or the kind of civil disobedience that paralyses entire communities, for true citizenship shares nothing of the extremist ideologies behind disruptive and destructive movements.

Rather, the six heretical ideas in these pages are meant to work together, incrementally but also cumulatively, and constructively, to increase our resilience as citizens, to help us be anything but paralysing forces, by providing real ways to strongly connect us to a place, and to each other, without violence and its evil siblings. If we can manage to do even some of the things in this book, we will increase our ability to adapt to even the worst-case scenarios, with solidarity and compassion. And maybe one day, with justice for all.

The sceptics will still ask whether it is really possible that our fanatical attachment to order has prevented us from having a 'good life' or at least has made it more difficult to achieve. Yes, I respond. Until we all truly feel the need to spontaneously create a dynamic order for ourselves, we will never sufficiently obey the order and rules imposed upon us from above. Thucydides, the great historian of Athens and Sparta, already had it right some four hundred years before Christ when he warned that human nature was 'always ready to offend even where laws exist'.[3] And, in saying this, I become a heretic in the world of law and order, a world that I have defended for decades. Because it is with human nature instead that we must begin and do the hard work. The potential is there.

My plan calls for action in all of these six areas, or pillars, which, taken together, can weave a supportive fabric of responsibility and form the basis for cooperative citizenship for us all. All of these pillars are united in their contribution to our friendly independence from the state *and* our dependence on one another. They overlap and they sustain each other—for as we fail in one area, we are likely to fail in the rest. The line between these pillars is not hard and fast, nor are the solutions. But when we start working to fix the problems in one area, one pillar of citizenship, we will be on the road to fixing problems in all.

Why don't we use this moment in our history as a catalyst to build real citizens, a true civil society, one that has never, could never, exist on a global level, until now? So when the next challenge comes (because it will, and soon), we can say, 'We've got this.' And we can mean it this time.

Acknowledgements

I HAVE SO MANY PEOPLE TO THANK FOR THE POSSIBILITY and realization of this book, and even more to blame. I must restrict myself here to only a few individual names or risk making this section longer than the text itself, though in truth it should be. I sincerely if inelegantly hope that those who know how and where they have helped me along my journey, concretely or otherwise, know how indebted to them and how grateful to them I really am. From the many students and colleagues I have had the privilege to work with over the years, to the legal experts, policy makers, and ordinary citizens who welcomed me into their spaces, narrated important tales that are found here, and shared and broke bread with me: thank you, all of you. Any errors of course remain my own.

Mark Tushnet read the entire manuscript and provided an important dialogue over the years. T. J. Kelleher at Basic Books, and Alexis Kirschbaum and Jasmine Horsey at Bloomsbury, believed enough in this project to take it on, and they and their teams then made it *so much better*. I am particularly grateful to the entire team at Basic, including Annie Chatham, Lara Heimert, Kristen Kim, Olivia Loperfido, and Carrie Watterson, and the entire team at Bloomsbury, including Akua Boateng, Ben Chisnall, Anna Massardi, Molly McCarthy, Nigel Newton, and Lauren Whybrow. But none of this would have been possible without my incredible agent, Emma Bal.

This book is dedicated to my children, Demara and Raphael, with gratitude for just being and for embracing my unorthodox approach to just about everything. It is for them, for their generation of young citizens and those to come, in the hope of a more cooperative life, that I plant these modest seeds.

Notes

Preface

1. The literature on federalism, its pros and cons and varieties, is vast. One of the supporters of asymmetrical federalism, based on his research in India and elsewhere, was Alfred Stepan; see his 'Federalism and Democracy: Beyond the US Model', *Journal of Democracy*, Vol. 10, No. 4, 1999.

2. Some of the influential work on Spanish devolution and its link with democracy is found in Juan J. Linz and Alfred Stepan, *Problems of Democratic Transition and Consolidation: Southern Europe, South America and Post-Communist Europe*, Johns Hopkins University Press, Baltimore, 1996.

3. This lengthy yet non-comprehensive list details attacks in Iraq in 2009–2010, the period of my work there: https://www.refworld.org/pdfid/517521334.pdf.

4. Others have raised issues and concerns with legal transplants, including Vlad Perju, 'Constitutional Transplants: Borrowing and Migrations', in M. Rosenfeld and A. Sajó (eds.), *The Oxford Handbook of Comparative Constitutional Law*, Oxford University Press, Oxford, 2012, pp. 1304–1327.

Introduction

1. Alfred Stepan and Cindy Skach, 'Constitutional Frameworks and Democratic Consolidation: Parliamentarianism versus Presidentialism', *World Politics*, Vol. 46, No. 1, October 1993, pp. 1–22. We provided some of the first evidence, but it was Juan Linz at Yale University who first began writing and presenting papers that provoked our research. Other work supporting these claims included Adam Przeworski, with Michael E. Alvarez, Jose Antonio Cheibub, and Fernando Limongi, *Democracy and Development: Political Institutions and Well-Being in the World, 1950–1990*, Cambridge University Press, Cambridge, 2000. Some scholars disagreed with our

line of argument and correlations, including Jose Antonio Cheibub, 'Presidentialism and Democratic Performance', in Andrew Reynolds (ed.), *The Architecture of Democracy: Constitutional Design, Conflict Management, and Democracy*, Oxford University Press, Oxford, 2002.

2. See the Gini index at the World Bank Poverty and Inequality Platform, data.worldbank.org. For comparison, Brazil's coefficient in 2021 was 52.9, France in 2020 was 30.7, Norway 27.7 in 2019, the UK 32.6 in 2020, and the US 39.7 in 2020.

3. Here see the work of Paulo Sergio Pinheiro, Brazilian legal scholar and former secretary of state for human rights under President Fernando Henrique Cardoso's administration.

4. As discussed in my *Borrowing Constitutional Designs: Constitutional Law in Weimar Germany and the French Fifth Republic*, Princeton University Press, Princeton, NJ, 2005.

5. Examples include M. Rainer Lepsius, a German sociologist and scholar with particular interest in Max Weber, German nationalism, and the rise of the National Socialists.

6. My interview with her is detailed in my 'Russia's Constitutional Dictatorship: A Brief History', *University of Miami International and Comparative Law Review*, Vol. 29, No. 1, 2021.

7. Guillermo A. O'Donnell, 'Delegative Democracy', *Journal of Democracy*, Vol. 5, No. 1, 1994, pp. 55–69.

8. Some of this is detailed in publications by the European Roma Rights Centre. See, for example, 'Hungary: What's Actually New About Viktor Orbán's Latest Racist Outburst?', ERRC, 29 July 2022, www.errc.org/news/hungary-whats-actually-new-about-viktor-orbans-latest-racist-outburst.

9. A telling account which outlines the long-term positive effects of the Arab Spring are found in Noah Feldman, *The Arab Winter: A Tragedy*, Princeton University Press, Princeton, NJ, 2020.

10. See Paolo Maurizio Talanti's compelling article 'Alika Is Our George Floyd', *Vogue Italia*, 2 August 2022.

11. For a recent historical excavation of papers relating to mental health, psychology, and leadership, see Patrick Weil, *The Madman in the White House*, Harvard University Press, Cambridge, MA, 2023.

12. https://worldjusticeproject.org/rule-of-law-index/. Data from the World Justice Project on the rule of law which evaluated 140 countries and jurisdictions around the world and in 2022 declared backsliding for most of the countries in this set of 140 measured according to their indicators for the rule of law; these included how accountable leaders were, how just and clear

the laws were, how well constraints on government power worked, and the absence of corruption.

13. Organisation for Economic Co-operation and Development (OECD), OECD Trust in Government Survey 2021. This survey, which canvassed the opinion of some fifty thousand citizens across twenty-two OECD countries, found that trust and distrust in government are evenly split, with 41.4 per cent stating they trust their national government, and 41.1 per cent saying they do not. See www.oecd.org/newsroom/governments-seen -as-reliable-post-pandemic-but-giving-citizens-greater-voice-is-critical-to -strengthening-trust.htm.

14. See Ipsos, 'Interpersonal Trust Across the World', March 2022 www.ipsos.com/sites/default/files/ct/news/documents/2022-03/Global Advisor–Interpersonal Trust 2022–Graphic Report_0.pdf; inhabitants of thirty countries were polled.

15. See, for example, the work of Steven Levitsky and Daniel Ziblatt, *How Democracies Die*, Crown, New York, 2018; or Ed Miliband, *Go Big: How to Fix Our World*, Bodley Head, London, 2021.

16. See the data in Freedom House, 'Freedom in the World 2023: Marking 50 Years in the Struggle for Democracy', https://freedomhouse.org/sites /default/files/2023-03/FIW_World_2023_DigtalPDF.pdf.

17. Bill Chappell, 'Protesting Racism Versus Risking COVID-19: "I Wouldn't Weigh These Crises Separately"', NPR News, 1 June 2020.

18. Thomas Hobbes, *Leviathan or The Matter, Forme and Power of a Commonwealth Ecclesiasticall and Civil*, was published in 1651 and remains today a foundational text in political and legal theory.

Chapter One: Lessons from the Law

1. Much more nuance than I am able to detail here clearly exists in these narratives, for the creation myths across nations and cultures are all imbued with important linguistic, historical, subcultural, and other subtleties that specialists can decipher. On Korea, one of the most cited in the English language is Boudewijn Walraven. See in particular the book edited by Robert E. Buswell Jr, *Religions of Korea in Practice*, Princeton University Press, Princeton, NJ, 2007, which includes essays by Walraven and others.

2. See, for example, John Bierhorst, *The Mythology of Mexico and Central America*, William Morrow, New York, 1990.

3. See the fascinating Samuel Noah Kramer, *History Begins at Sumer: Thirty-Nine Firsts in Recorded History*, University of Pennsylvania Press, Philadelphia, 1988.

4. S. E. Merry, 'Law: Anthropological Aspects', in Neil J. Smelser and Paul B. Baltes (eds.), *International Encyclopedia of the Social and Behavioural Sciences*, Pergamon Press, Oxford, 2001.

5. This is at least the perspective of Ronald M. Dworkin, 'The Model of Rules', *University of Chicago Law Review*, Vol. 35, No. 14, 1967–68, pp. 14–46. To go further, see the published debate between Lon Fuller and H. L. A. Hart in the *Harvard Law Review*: H. L. A. Hart, 'Positivism and the Separation of Law and Morals', *Harvard Law Review*, Vol. 71, No. 4, 1958, pp. 593–629; and Lon L. Fuller, 'Positivism and Fidelity to Law—a Reply to Professor Hart', *Harvard Law Review*, Vol. 71, No. 4, 1958, pp. 630–672.

6. Douglas C. North, Nobel laureate in economics, was perhaps the first to refer to laws as humanly devised constraints, in his article 'Institutions', *Journal of Economic Perspectives*, Vol. 5, No. 1, Winter 1991, pp. 97–112.

7. One important discussion of constitutionalism, as a concept, is found in Charles Howard McIlwain, *Constitutionalism: Ancient and Modern*, Cornell University Press, Ithaca, NY, 1947.

8. This is a broad-stroke classification, taken from the more detailed timeline which can be seen at https://comparativeconstitutionsproject.org/chronology/; as well as in Zachary Elkins, Tom Ginsburg, and James Melton, *The Endurance of National Constitutions*, Cambridge University Press, New York, 2009.

9. Cicero, *On Obligations*, translated by P. G. Walsh, Oxford University Press, Oxford, 2000, quote from Book 3, paragraphs 26–28.

10. Reinhard Zimmermann, *The Law of Obligations: Roman Foundations of the Civilian Tradition*, Clarendon Press, Oxford, 1996.

11. I remain grateful to Robert Amdur for alerting me to this episode and its important connection to my point here.

12. See Proudhon's *General Idea of the Revolution in the Nineteenth Century*, translated by John Beverley Robinson, Anodos Books, Whithorn, 2018, p. 240.

13. See, to begin with, Michael Polanyi, *The Logic of Liberty*, University of Chicago Press, Chicago, 1951.

14. *The Book of Chuang Tzu*, Penguin Books, London, 2006.

15. Or what Donald Lutz prefers to call 'self-preservation, unfettered sociability, and beneficial innovation'. See his Principles of Constitutional Design, Cambridge University Press, New York, 2006; and Walter F. Murphy, *Constitutional Democracy: Creating and Maintaining a Just Political Order*, Johns Hopkins University Press, Baltimore, 2007; as well as my

review of their work in the *International Journal of Constitutional Law*, Vol. 7, No. 1, January 2009, pp. 175–181.

16. See the arguments in Michael C. Dorf, 'The Aspirational Constitution', *George Washington Law Review*, Vol. 77, Nos. 5/6, September 2009, pp. 1631–1671; or Frank Michelman, 'Socioeconomic Rights in Constitutional Law: Explaining America Away', *International Journal of Constitutional Law*, Vol. 6, Nos. 3/4, July–October 2008, pp. 663–686.

17. Charles Tilly, *Stories, Identities, and Political Change*, Rowman & Littlefield, Lanham, MD, 2002.

18. Ellen M. Immergut, 'Institutions, Veto Points, and Policy Results: A Comparative Analysis of Health Care', *Journal of Public Policy*, Vol. 10, No. 4, 1990, pp. 391–416.

19. First aired in 1979, performed by Lynn Ahrens. A clarification decades later states that 'this segment on our government's system of checks and balances was made but not aired for several years out of concern that some politicians might be offended by the circus analogy'. See Tom Yohe and George Newall, *Schoolhouse Rock! The Updated Official Guide*, Hyperion, Los Angeles, 2023.

20. The real origin of the quote is disputed; see Steven Luxenberg, 'A Likely Story . . . and That's Precisely the Problem', *Washington Post*, 17 April 2005.

Chapter Two: Don't Play Follow the Leader

1. This is not to ignore the catalytic work that had been done to encourage women to come forward, particularly the award-winning investigative work of *New York Times* reporters Jodi Kantor and Megan Twohey, collected and published as *She Said: Breaking the Sexual Harassment Story That Helped Ignite a Movement*, Penguin Press, New York, 2019.

2. See the account at 'Grenoble: L'acte héroïque des habitants d'un quartier pour sauver deux enfants des flammes', *Le Dauphine Libere*, 21 July 2020, www.ledauphine.com/faits-divers-justice/2020/07/21 /grenoble-deux-enfants-sautent-d-un-balcon-pour-echapper-a-un-incendie.

3. Zeynep Tufekci, *Twitter and Tear Gas: The Power and Fragility of Networked Protest*, Yale University Press, New Haven, CT, 2017.

4. Jim Newton, 'City Hall's Embrace of Occupy L.A.', *Los Angeles Times*, 20 March 2014, www.latimes.com/opinion/opinion-la/la-oe -newton-column-occupy-la-and-the-city-council-20111024-column.html.

5. Here I note the pioneering work of Frances Haugen and Sophie Zhang, two brave data scientists who exposed some of the problems with

social media and called for greater oversight. At first glance their calls for greater regulation appear to clash with my move away from such control, yet perhaps it can be consistent: save the rules, regulations, and oversight for those elements of our society, such as corporations, most likely to abuse their privileged places, leaving the self-organising, spontaneous work of everyday life to the rest of us.

6. Susanne Lohmann, 'The Dynamics of Informational Cascades: The Monday Demonstrations in Leipzig, East Germany, 1989–91', *World Politics*, 47, October 1994, pp. 42–101.

7. In the social sciences there are important theories and debates about how this all happens, whether there is an information cascade—a two-step process in which individuals first decide whether they are going to act, and then after observing others who acted before them, they act; or whether it is herd mentality. Obviously during crisis periods, the question of why individuals act against their own rationality (for example, when they might be injured or arrested) makes us pause to ask what is driving them, and whether there is something more to human beings' desire for self-preservation than meets the eye. This is where we and the bubbles might diverge, because information cascades, like bubbles, can be modelled with mathematical formulae, whereas we, unlike the bubbles, have emotions which may make us behave in ways that cannot be predicted by mathematics but that still might be rational.

8. Charles E. Fritz, 'Disasters and Mental Health: Therapeutic Principles Drawn from Disaster Studies', University of Delaware Disaster Research Center, Series No. 10, 1996. The paper was written in 1961, but for various reasons explained in the preface it was not published until thirty-five years later.

9. Fritz, 'Disasters and Mental Health', p. 4.

10. For the value of emergency powers, and a nuanced discussion that includes Machiavelli's defence of Roman dictatorship, see John Ferejohn and Pasquale Pasquino, 'The Law of the Exception: A Typology of Emergency Powers', *I.CON*, Vol. 2, No. 2, 2004, pp. 210–239.

11. See Steven M. Southwick, Brett T. Litz, Dennis Charney, and Matthew J. Friedman (eds.), *Resilience and Mental Health: Challenges Across the Lifespan*, Cambridge University Press, Cambridge, 2011; and the nuanced discussion in Amanda R. Carrico, Heather Barnes Truelove, and Nicholas E. Williams, 'Social Capital and Resilience to Drought Among Smallholding Farmers in Sri Lanka', *Climate Change*, Vol. 155, 2019, pp. 195–213. Also see G. T. Svendsen and G. L. Svendsen, eds., *Handbook of Social*

Capital: The Troika of Sociology, Political Science and Economics, Edward Elgar, Northampton, MA, 2008.

12. Rebecca Solnit, *A Paradise Built in Hell: The Extraordinary Communities That Arise in Disaster*, Penguin, New York, 2009, p. 312.

13. This was the way privacy was described famously by legal scholars Samuel Warren and Louis Brandeis in their 'The Right to Privacy', *Harvard Law Review*, Vol. 4, No. 5, pp. 193–220, December 1890.

14. 'Delay to Free School Meal Extension "Shameful", EIS Union Says', BBC, 27 December 2022, www.bbc.co.uk/news/uk-scotland -64095765.amp.

15. See the study published in 2022 by Rebecca O'Connell at University College London in the UK, and her colleagues in Lisbon and Norway: Rebecca O'Connell, Julia Brannen, Vasco Ramos, Silje Skuland, and Monica Truninger, 'School Meals as a Resource for Low-Income Families in Three European Countries: A Comparative Case Approach', *European Societies*, Vol. 24, No. 3, 2022, pp. 251–282.

16. See the statistics quoted from government documents on their website, Oxfordfoodhub.org.

17. One proponent of this form of democratic experimentalism is Hélène Landemore, *Open Democracy: Reinventing Popular Rule for the Twenty-First Century*, Princeton University Press, Princeton, NJ, 2020. Also see the discussion in Jane Mansbridge, Joshua Cohen, Daniela Cammack, Peter Stone, Christopher H. Achen, Ethan J. Leib, and Hélène Landemore, 'Representing and Being Represented in Turn—a Symposium on Hélène Landemore's *Open Democracy*', *Journal of Deliberative Democracy*, Vol. 18, No. 1, 2022, pp. 1–12.

18. See Cristina Lafont, *Democracy Without Shortcuts: A Participatory Conception of Deliberative Democracy*, Oxford University Press, Oxford, 2020; as well as Robert Goodin's critique, 'Between Full Endorsement and Blind Deference', *Journal of Deliberative Democracy*, Vol. 16, No. 2, 2020, pp. 25–32.

19. J. Holt-Lunstad, T. B. Smith, and J. B. Layton, 'Social Relationships and Mortality Risk: A Meta-analytic Review', *PLOS Medicine*, Vol. 7, No. 7, 27 July 2010, e1000316, doi: 10.1371/journal.pmed.1000316.

20. See Dunbar's presentation, 'Friendship and Social Relationships: Understanding the Power of Our Most Important Relationships', 27 January 2021, Webinar Series of the Evolutionary Psychiatry Section of the World Psychiatric Association, https://www.youtube.com

/watch?v=4ya1o5TX73M. Also see "Don't Believe Facebook: You Only Have 150 Friends," *All Things Considered*, NPR, 5 June 2011.

21. A classic work on this is James Gleick, *Chaos*, Vintage, London, 1997; also see Melanie Mitchell, *Complexity: A Guided Tour*, Oxford University Press, New York, 2011.

22. One of the first to do so was the brilliant John von Neumann, not of the Guinness bubbles per se but of a two-dimensional foam structure. See his 1952 discussion in *Metal Interfaces*, the journal of the American Society for Metals, in Cleveland, OH, pp. 108–110.

23. Some important histories include Karl Dietrich Bracher, *The German Dictatorship: The Origins, Structure and Consequences of National Socialism*, Penguin Books, Harmondsworth, 1991.

24. Cindy Skach, *Borrowing Constitutional Designs*, Princeton University Press, Princeton, NJ, 2005.

25. There is an important, long-standing debate on the relationship between law and morality. My point is not to exhaust it here, but one of the contemporary contributors to this debate who engages important, recent examples is the South African / Canadian jurist David Dyzenhaus. See, for example, his *Hard Cases in Wicked Legal Systems: Pathologies of Legality*, Oxford University Press, Oxford, 2010.

Chapter Three: Own Your Rights, but Responsibly

1. French anthropologist Annie Lebeuf was one of the first female anthropologists to appreciate the nuances of matriarchy in Africa and bring it more directly into academic discourse.

2. Charlie Savage of the *New York Times* found and published some of Kagan's memos, including the one critical to this case, in his article of 3 June 2010, 'In Supreme Court Work, Early Views of Kagan'.

3. Robert M. Cover, 'Violence and the Word', *Yale Law Journal*, Vol. 95, No. 8, July 1986, pp. 1601–1629.

4. Lon L. Fuller, 'The Case of the Speluncean Explorers', *Harvard Law Review*, Vol. 62, No. 4, February 1949, pp. 616–645.

5. 'Boy Who Refused Blood Transfusion Dies', CBS News, 30 November 2007, www.cbsnews.com/news/boy-who-refused-blood-transfusion-dies/.

6. See Joan Kron, 'As Karen Ann Quinlan Lives On in a Coma, a New Book and TV Film Tell Her Story', *New York Times*, 24 September 1977, p. 10.

7. 'Muslim Girl Shaves Head over Ban', BBC, 1 October 2004.

8. A good overview of their function as well as the appropriate literature, discussing Hans Kelsen, legal theorist and architect of the Austrian Constitutional Court, is Nuno Garoupa and Tom Ginsburg, 'Building Reputation in Constitutional Courts: Political and Judicial Audiences', *Arizona Journal of International and Comparative Law*, Vol. 28, No. 3, 2011, pp. 539–568.

9. Here the analogy of the prisoner's dilemma, and in particular the role that values play in decisions to cooperate or defect, is instructive. See, for example, Derek Parfit, 'Prudence, Morality, and the Prisoner's Dilemma', Annual Philosophical Lecture, Henriette Hertz Trust, 1978. Importantly, in the PD, the prisoners cannot communicate with one another, and this is a critical difference because they cannot know what the other will choose to do.

10. See Vanda Felbab-Brown, 'Conceptualizing Crime as Competition in State-Making and Designing an Effective Response', Brookings Institution, commentary, 21 May 2010. Also see Charles Tilly, 'War Making and State Making as Organized Crime', in Peter Evans, Dietrich Rueschemeyer, and Theda Skocpol (eds.), *Bringing the State Back In*, Cambridge University Press, Cambridge, 1985, pp. 169–191.

11. ... *And Justice for All*, Columbia Pictures, 1979.

12. See Michael Sandel, *Justice: What's the Right Thing to Do?*, Farrar, Straus and Giroux, New York, 2009, which was based on his popular undergraduate course.

13. House of Lords, 'Judgments—Oxfordshire County Council (Respondents) v. Oxford City Council (Appellants) and Another (Respondent) (2005) and Others', session 2005–2006, https://publications.parliament.uk /pa/ld200506/ldjudgmt/jd060524/oxf-1.htm.

14. Not in my backyard. Such questions are clearly complex, with decent and less decent arguments on both sides, but they all illustrate the problem of respecting others' rights. Many of the sides in these NIMBY problems fail to appreciate the others' perspectives, perhaps because these problems tend to be structured as zero-sum issues with clear winners and losers. See a recent take in Conor Dougherty, 'Twilight of the NIMBY', *New York Times*, 5 June 2022, www.nytimes.com/2022/06/05/business/economy /california-housing-crisis-nimby.html.

15. Reg Little, 'Anger at Nature of Trap Grounds', *Oxford Mail*, 14 January 2009.

16. Yasminah Beebeejaun, 'Gender, Urban Space, and the Right to Everyday Life', *Journal of Urban Affairs*, Vol. 39, No. 3, 2017, pp. 323–334. Also see her edited volume, *The Participatory City*, Jovis Verlag, Berlin, 2016.

17. The Federal Constitutional Court in Germany has come up with one of several examples of potentially creative solutions to the controversial issue of abortion. Having to satisfy both the Christian majority in Germany and, after reunification, the East Germans who had lived for decades with a different and in some ways more progressive understanding of abortion, the court in 1993 adjudicated that abortion is not legal, but it is also under certain conditions not punishable.

18. See some of the attempts to control this in Anna Jobin, Marcello Lenca, and Effy Vayena, 'The Global Landscape of AI Ethics Guidelines', *Nature Machine Intelligence*, September 2019.

19. https://www.climavore.org.

20. See the fascinating experiments detailed and analyzed in Nikos Papastergiadis (ed.), *Ambient Screens and Transnational Public Spaces*, Hong Kong, 2016, online ed., Hong Kong Scholarship Online, 21 September 2017, with special thanks to Carrie Watterson.

21. Benedict Anderson, *Imagined Communities*, Verso, New York, 1983, p. 35.

22. See Albert Hirschman, *Strategy of Economic Development*, Yale University Press, New Haven, CT, 1958.

23. See the account by Maria Cramer, 'What Happened When a Brooklyn Neighborhood Policed Itself for Five Days', *New York Times*, 4 June 2023.

24. See the details on https://camba.org.

25. Robert A. Dahl, *Polyarchy: Participation and Opposition*, Yale University Press, New Haven, CT, 1971.

26. My former colleagues Steven Levitsky and Daniel Ziblatt are examples of scholars who have focused on institutions and institutional practices. As important as they might be, I nevertheless feel the answers do not lie there. See both their *How Democracies Die*, Crown, New York, 2018, and the equally important review by historian David Runciman, *Guardian*, 24 January 2018.

27. Amos Tversky and Daniel Kahneman, 'The Framing of Decisions and the Psychology of Choice', *Science*, Vol. 211, January 1981, pp. 453–458.

28. Economist James Andreoni was one of the first to use the term 'warm glow giving'. See, for example, his 'Giving with Impure Altruism', *Journal of Political Economy*, Vol. 97, No. 6, 1989, pp. 1447–1458.

29. Rutger Bregman, *Humankind: A Hopeful History*, trans. Erica Moore and Elizabeth Manton, New York, Little, Brown and Company, 2020.

30. In the United States, see *Masterpiece Cakeshop v Colorado Civil Rights Commission*, decided 4 June 2018. In the UK, see *Lee v Ashers Baking Company*, judgement given on 10 October 2018.

31. Interview with me by Messenger, 11 February 2022.

Chapter Four: Hang Out in a Piazza, Repeatedly

1. Jürgen Habermas, 'The Public Sphere: An Encyclopedia Article (1964)', translated by Sara Lennox and Frank Lennox, *New German Critique*, No. 3, 1974, pp. 49–55.

2. For one of the more vivid accounts linking the past to the present day, see Adrian Rennix and Sparky Abraham, 'Trial by Combat and the Myths of Our Modern Legal System', *Current Affairs*, February 2021, www .currentaffairs.org/2021/02/trial-by-combat-and-the-myths-of-our -modern-legal-system; as well as Ariella Elema, 'Trial by Battle in France and England', the medievalist's doctoral thesis submitted to the University of Toronto in 2012, from which they draw.

3. Rennix and Abraham, 'Trial by Combat'.

4. John Marshall, 'Lawyers, Truth and the Zero-Sum Game', *Notre Dame Law Review*, Vol. 47, No. 4, 1972, p. 919.

5. See both the majority and dissenting opinions of the Supreme Court of the United States, *Dobbs v Jackson*, No. 19–1392, decided 24 June 2022, at www.supremecourt.gov/opinions/21pdf/19-1392_6j37.pdf.

6. In some areas of law, there has been a gradual and steady move towards mediation, as the zero-sum court battles, delays, and other characteristics of the legal route frustrate many on all sides.

7. Bertolt Brecht and Margarete Steffin, *Mother Courage and Her Children*, 1939, in particular see the annotated student edition, Bertolt Brecht, John Willett, and Hugh Rorrison, *Mother Courage and Her Children*, Bloomsbury, London, 2015.

8. Richard Fusch, 'The Piazza in Italian Urban Morphology', *Geographical Review*, October 1994, quote from p. 424.

9. See David Harvey's interesting talk at the CCCB, www.cccb.org/en /multimedia/videos/david-harvey-i-like-the-idea-of-an-urban-common -which-is-a-political-concept-which-says-that-this-space-is-open-for-all -kind-of-people/229344.

10. The story of the Mangrove is the focus of the first episode of visual artist Steve McQueen's recent Small Axe series on Amazon.

11. Robin Bunce and Paul Field, 'Mangrove Nine: The Court Challenge Against Police Racism in Notting Hill', *Guardian*, 29 November 2010.

12. See the detailed account in Robin Bunce and Paul Field, *Renegade: The Life and Times of Darcus Howe*, Bloomsbury, London, 2021.

13. Neil Kenlock, interview with the author by email via Emelia Kenlock, 23 November 2020.

14. Something known as the Trojan Horse scandal, or Birmingham schools controversy, of 2014 continues to be debated by journalists, politicians, and residents alike. One recent take is offered by Sonia Sodha, 'The Trojan Horse Affair: How *Serial* Podcast Got It So Wrong', *Guardian*, Opinion, 20 February 2022.

15. https://skateboardgb.org/habito-skateboard-gb-grassroots -skatespaces.

16. British Academy, 'The COVID Decade: Understanding the Long-Term Societal Impacts of COVID-19', 2021, www.thebritishacademy .ac.uk/documents/3238/COVID-decade-understanding-long -term-societal-impacts-COVID-19.pdf.

17. This is the title of Bob Putnam's study of the decline of American associational life and its consequences for democracy. See his *Bowling Alone: The Collapse and Revival of American Community*, Simon & Schuster, New York, 2000.

18. Michael Chwe's own website has numerous links to this and more of his work, including his book, *Rational Ritual*, Princeton University Press, Princeton, NJ, 2001. See http://chwe.net/michael/.

19. Michael Chwe, 'Social Media Enhances the Power of "Common Knowledge"', *UCLA Faculty Voice*, https://newsroom.ucla.edu/stories /ucla-faculty-voice-social-media-enhances-the-power-of-common-knowledge.

20. More about the project can be found at www.mycallisto.org.

21. Robert Putnam, with Robert Leonardi and Raffaella Nanetti, *Making Democracy Work: Civic Traditions in Modern Italy*, Princeton University Press, Princeton, NJ, 1993.

22. Sheri Berman, 'Civil Society and the Collapse of the Weimar Republic', *World Politics*, April 1997.

23. Habermas, 'Public Sphere'.

24. See Thorstein Veblen, *The Theory of the Leisure Class*, Macmillan, New York, 1899.

25. Leslie Kern's work aims not only to identify the problems but also suggest solutions. See her *Feminist City: Claiming Space in the Man-Made World*, Verso, London, 2020.

26. Krista Schroeder, Jennie G. Noll, Kevin A. Henry, Shakira F. Suglia, and David B. Sarwer, 'Trauma-Informed Neighborhoods: Making the Built Environment Trauma-Informed', *Preventive Medicine Reports*, 2021, www.sciencedirect.com/science/article/pii/S22113 35521001911?ref=pdf_download&fr=RR-9&rr=83ebefba39d471db.

27. Here the work on capabilities by Amartya Sen and Martha Nussbaum has certainly inspired my ideas; see their *The Quality of Life*, Clarendon Press, Oxford, 1993.

28. E. L. Sweet (ed.), *Disassembled Cities: Spatial, Social and Conceptual Trajectories Across the Urban Globe*, Routledge, London, 2019.

29. See, for example, the World Health Organisation news release, 'COVID-19 Pandemic Triggers 25% Increase in Prevalence of Anxiety and Depression Worldwide', 2 March 2022.

30. Alain Corbin, *A History of Silence: From the Renaissance to the Present Day*, translated by Jean Birrell, Polity Press, Cambridge, MA, 2018, quote from the preface of the Kindle edition.

31. Corbin, *A History of Silence*.

32. See Michael Sandel's discussion of Aristotle in his *Justice*, particularly Chapter 8.

33. D. Platts-Fowler and D. Robinson, 'Community Resilience: A Policy Tool for Local Government?', *Local Government Studies*, Vol. 42, No. 5, 2016, pp. 762–784.

34. Centers for Disease Control and Prevention, 'Violence Prevention: Risk and Protective Factors', www.cdc.gov/violenceprevention/aces/risk protectivefactors.html.

35. On this idea of embodiment, think of the work of Antonio Damásio, or more recently Andy Clark. See Clark's ideas as critically engaged by Larissa MacFarquhar, 'The Mind-Expanding Ideas of Andy Clark', *New Yorker*, 26 March 2018.

36. Austin Sarat, 'Situating Law Between the Realities of Violence and the Claims of Justice', in Sarat (ed.), *Law, Violence, and the Possibility of Justice*, Princeton University Press, Princeton, NJ, 2001, p. 3.

Chapter Five: Grow Your Own Tomatoes, and Share Them

1. See *Suray Prasad Sharma Dhungerl v Godawari Marble Industries*, Supreme Court of Nepal, 31 October 1995.

2. A fascinating study of raw milk in the United States and in Vermont in particular is found in the doctoral thesis by Andrea M. Suozzo, 'Pasteurization and Its Discontents: Raw Milk, Risk, and the Reshaping of the Dairy Industry', University of Vermont, 2015.

3. Nearing's project was not without criticism. See his and his wife's version in Scott Nearing and Helen Nearing, *The Good Life*, Schocken Books, New York, 1989.

4. Leah Penniman, *Farming While Black: Soul Fire Farm's Practical Guide to Liberation on the Land*, Chelsea Green, White River Junction, VT, 2018.

5. Isabella Tree, *Wilding: The Return of Nature to a British Farm*, Picador, London, 2018.

6. Examples are found everywhere, but take one case as complex as that of the Banat region in Romania. Here researchers have shown that 'the local ethno-cultural diversity has lasted for about 250 years in Timis County and in the whole Banat region, without having undergone conflicts or deep structural reshuffles. . . . This diversity is animated by coexistence, co-participation and intercultural exchanges, with the preservation of local identities and regional plurality. This creates the conditions for ensuring equity in the social life of local authorities and for participating in decision-making, regardless of culture or ethnicity.' See the data in Iancu-Constantin Berceanu and Nicolae Popa, 'A Sample of Resilient Intercultural Coexistence in Ethnic Hungarian, Serbian and Bulgarian Communities in Western Romania', *Social Sciences*, Vol. 11, No. 8, 2022, quote from p. 21, https://mdpi-res.com/d_attachment/socsci/socsci-11-00320/article _deploy/socsci-11-00320.pdf?version=1658483204.

7. Nina Lakhani, Aliya Uteuova, and Alvin Chang, 'Revealed: The True Extent of America's Food Monopolies, and Who Pays the Price', *Guardian*, 14 July 2021, www.theguardian.com/environment/ng-interactive/2021 /jul/14/food-monopoly-meals-profits-data-investigation.

8. Taylor Telford, Kimberly Kindy, and Jacob Bogage, 'Trump Orders Meat Plant to Stay Open in Pandemic', *Washington Post*, 29 April 2020, www.washingtonpost.com/business/2020/04/28/trump-meat-plants-dpa/.

9. Nina Lakhani, 'Trump Officials and Meat Industry Blocked Life-Saving COVID Controls, Investigation Finds', *Guardian*, 12 May 2022.

10. See the Edible Cutteslowe Facebook page at https://www.facebook .com/ediblecutteslowe.

11. Elizabeth A. Harris, 'The Museum Is Closed, but Its Tomato Man Soldiers On', *New York Times*, 17 May 2020.

12. André Béranger's Last Battle in the Villeneuve, letter. In homage from the Popular Urbanism Workshop to Béranger, published on the Global Platform for the Right to the City, www.right2city.org/news /andre-berangers-last-battle-in-the-villeneuve/.

13. Rem Koolhaas quoted in Chris Michael, '"Lagos Shows How a City Can Recover from a Deep, Deep Pit": Rem Koolhaas Talks to Kunlé Adeyemi', *Guardian*, 26 February 2016.

14. Penniman, *Farming While Black*.
15. Assemble, 'Granby Four Streets 2013', https://assemblestudio.co.uk /projects/granby-four-streets-2.
16. Assemble, 'Granby Workshop 2015', https://assemblestudio.co.uk /projects/granby-workshop.
17. Nathalie Pettorelli, Sarah M. Durant, and Johan T. du Toit (eds.), *Rewilding*, Cambridge University Press, Cambridge, 2019.
18. Pettorelli, Durant, and du Toit (eds.), *Rewilding*.
19. National Research Council, *The Public Health Effects of Food Deserts: Workshop Summary*, National Academies Press, Washington, DC, 2009.
20. '"The Pharmacist Will See You Now": Use Community Pharmacists Differently to Reduce Pressures on GPs', Press Release, University of Bath, 12 July 2023.

Chapter Six: Eat 'Ethnic Food', Regularly

1. Michael Walzer, *On Toleration*, Yale University Press, New Haven, CT, 1999.
2. See, for example, Michelle Alexander's *The New Jim Crow: Mass Incarceration in the Age of Colourblindness*, Penguin, London, 2019.
3. Department for Digital, Culture, Media & Sport and Nadine Dorries, 'New Poll Finds 7 in 10 Adults Want Social Media Firms to Do More to Tackle Harmful Content', 12 July 2022, www.gov.uk/government /news/new-poll-finds-7-in-10-adults-want-social-media-firms-to-do-more -to-tackle-harmful-content.
4. Ernest Gellner, *Nations and Nationalism*, New York University Press, New York, 1998.
5. Nicholas Sambanis, 'Ethnic Partition as a Solution to Ethnic War: An Empirical Critique of the Theoretical Literature', World Bank, 21 June 2013.
6. Elizabeth V. Spelman and Martha Minow, 'Outlaw Women: An Essay on Thelma & Louise', *New England Law Review*, Vol. 26, Summer 1992, pp. 1281–1296, quote from p. 1281.
7. See Spelman and Minow, 'Outlaw Women'.
8. See Keir Monteith KC et al., 'Racial Bias and the Bench: A Response to the Judicial Diversity and Inclusion Strategy (2020–2025)', University of Manchester, November 2022.
9. Globally, public opinion in 2015 was divided, with about one-third of individuals saying immigration should decrease, one-third saying it should remain the same, and one-third saying it should increase. See the 'Public

Opinion on Migration', Migration Data Portal, updated 13 April 2021, www.migrationdataportal.org/themes/public-opinion-migration.

10. A terrific exploration is James Attlee, *Isolarion: A Different Oxford Journey*, Black Swan, London, 2009.

11. Craig R. Whitney, 'Rightists Play Immigrant Card in French Town', *New York Times*, 16 June 1995.

12. See James D. Fearon and David D. Laitin, 'Explaining Interethnic Cooperation', *American Political Science Review*, Vol. 90, No. 4, December 1996, pp. 715–735.

13. Judith Tendler, *Good Government in the Tropics*, Johns Hopkins University Press, Baltimore, 1997.

14. Prerna Singh, *How Solidarity Works for Welfare: Subnationalism and Social Development in India*, Cambridge University Press, Cambridge, 2016.

15. See Laidre's account in 'The Social Lives of Hermits', *Natural History*, n.d., www.naturalhistorymag.com/features/122719/the-social-lives -of-hermits.

16. Thomas C. Schelling, 'Models of Segregation', *American Economic Review*, Vol. 59, No. 2, pp. 488–493.

17. See her opinion in Jack M. Balkin (ed.), *What 'Brown v. Board of Education' Should Have Said*, New York University Press, New York, 2001.

18. Balkin, *What 'Brown v. Board of Education' Should Have Said*, p. 199.

Chapter Seven: Start This All Very Early, About Age Three

1. See the powerful speech by Kimberly Jones, 'The Social Contract Is Broken!', YouTube video, posted by David Jones Media, June 1, 2020, https://youtu.be/sb9_qGOa9Go?si=8F37zpO-v5UXJb27.

2. See the data presented by Jaime Saavedra, Sheena Fazili, Yi Ning Wong, Koen Geven, and Marie-Helene Cloutier, 'New Literacy Data Shines a Spotlight on Learning Crisis', World Bank Blogs, 16 May 2023, https://blogs .worldbank.org/education/new-literacy-data-shines-spotlight-learning-crisis.

3. Email exchange, 3 July 2023. See James Handscome, *A School Built on Ethos: Ideas, Assemblies and Hard-Won Wisdom*, Crown House, Carmarthen, UK, 2021.

4. Reggio Children, 'Reggio Emilia Approach: Timeline', www .reggiochildren.it/en/reggio-emilia-approach/timeline-en/.

5. www.remida.org.

6. See Dan Olweus, Susan P. Limber, et al., *Olweus Bullying Prevention Program Teacher's Guide*, Hazelden, Center City, MN, 2007.

7. Olweus et al., *Olweus Bullying Prevention Program Teacher's Guide*, p. 89.

8. Vea Vecchi, *Art and Creativity in Reggio Emilia: Exploring the Role and Potential of Ateliers in Early Childhood Education*, Routledge, London, 2010, p. 53.

9. Vecchi, *Art and Creativity in Reggio Emilia*, p. 53.

10. Ethics Centre, 'Big Thinker: Martha Nussbaum', 22 August 2017, https://ethics.org.au/big-thinker-martha-nussbaum/.

11. 'Vienna', Make Space for Girls, www.makespaceforgirls.co.uk /case-studies/vienna.

12. See the discussion in Sondra R. Herman, 'Dialogue: Children, Feminism, and Power: Alva Myrdal and Swedish Reform, 1929–1956', *Journal of Women's History*, Vol. 4, No. 2, Fall 1992, pp. 82–112.

13. See 'The History of Adventure Play', www.adventureplay.org.uk /history_intro.htm.

14. www.koopadventureplayground.com/single-post/2020/01/27 /Opportunity-to-join-KOOPs-Team, accessed 13 August 2022.

15. Mariana Brussoni, Rebecca Gibbons, Casey Gray, Takuro Ishikawa, Ellen Beate Hansen Sandseter, Adam Bienenstock, Guylaine Chabot, Pamela Fuselli, Susan Herrington, Ian Janssen, et al., 'What Is the Relationship between Risky Outdoor Play and Health in Children? A Systematic Review', *International Journal of Environmental Research and Public Health*, Vol. 12, No. 6, 8 June 2015, https://mdpi-res.com/d_attachment/ijerph /ijerph-12-06423/article_deploy/ijerph-12-06423.pdf?version=1433762720.

16. See the published report at https://issuu.com/wendykrussell/docs /smap_report_131016_for_web_hs; also see the video of play in action at 'Sharing Memories of Adventure Playgrounds', YouTube video, uploaded by Wendy Russell, 28 January 2017.

17. Like the anthropologist Clifford Geertz, whose famous article on 'deep play' borrowed the idea from philosopher Jeremy Bentham. Essentially the play was 'deep' because the stakes were so high that a rational agent would not play them. Perhaps this is the key to understanding why a massive, deep reform of education has not yet happened. See his 'Notes on the Balinese Cockfight', in *The Interpretation of Cultures*, Basic Books, New York, 1973.

18. Eberhard Fuchs and Gabriele Flügge, 'Adult Neuroplasticity: More Than 40 Years of Research', *Neural Plasticity*, 2014, www.ncbi.nlm.nih.gov /pmc/articles/PMC4026979/pdf/NP2014-541870.pdf. One of the first to demonstrate neuroplasticity both in youth and in adult animal brains was

Mark Rosenzweig, whose work laid the foundation for much of the research done today in this area. An extraordinary, if controversial, personal account is also found in Norman Doidge, *The Brain That Changes Itself*, Penguin Books, London, 2008.

19. https://centerhealthyminds.org.

Conclusion

1. Some of his work was eventually published as Jonas Salk and Jonathan Salk, *A New Reality: Human Evolution for a Sustainable Future*, City Point Press, Stratford, CT, 2018.

2. Joel Hellman, 'Winners Take All: The Politics of Partial Reform in Post-Communist Transitions', *World Politics*, Vol. 50, No. 2, January 1998, pp. 203–234.

3. Thucydides, *History of the Peloponnesian War*, translated by Rex Warner with an introduction and notes by M. I. Finley, Penguin, London, 1954, quote from Book 3, paragraph 84.

Index

Index

Index

Index

Index

Index

Godawari Marble Industries, Nepal, 145–146
goodwill
  as democratic necessity, 173–174
  sharing resources with immigration populations, 174–175
Gorbachev, Mikhail, 11
governance
  as development in socially diverse areas, 180–181
  lottocracy and sortition, 66–68
  presidential and parliamentary systems, 13–14, 48–51
  See also democracy
Granby Four Streets, Liverpool, United Kingdom, 159–162
Greece, ancient
  creation of humans in Greek myth, 144
  origins of the piazza, 116
green space: land protection in Oxford, 93–95
Grenoble, France: Villanueva housing project, 53–54
Guardian report on food choices, 152–153
guerrilla constitutionalism, 98–104, 106–108
Guggenheim Museum, New York, 155–158
Guilty Bystander concept, 35–36, 202
Guinness, foam structures in, 70–72
gun laws, 147
gun violence: BIVO community policing model, 103–104

Habermas, Jürgen, 130–132
Haldane, Andrew, 55
Hamer, Fannie Lou, 158–159
harmonious equilibrium, 70–71
Harris Westminster Sixth Form, London, United Kingdom, 197–198
Harvey, David, 116–117
health and safety
  accountability for child abuse, 82–83
  the benefits of social relationships, 68–69

benefits of the Granby Four reclamation, 162
community provision of family planning, 96
Cure Violence public health model, 103–104
the health benefits of nature, 162–163
raw milk production and consumption, 147–148
trauma-informed neighbourhoods, 134
See also public health
Hegel, G. W. F., 100–101
Hellman, Joel, 219–220
hermit crabs, 181–183
hierarchical leadership
  charismatic leadership, 13
  early modern European view, 36–37
  failure during the COVID pandemic, 52–53
  Germany's Nazi Party, 72
  history of, 48
  law and law enforcement, 30
  moving outside of constitutions, 22
  moving toward self-sufficiency and self-organisation, 65–66
  See also constitutions and constitution building
high culture, 171–172
higher law, constitutional law as, 3–4
Hirschman, Albert, 102
Hobbes, Thomas, 21
homogeneous communities, 185
homogenisation in state building, 171–173
horizontal relationships
  BIVO links, 104
  children's playspaces, 212
  defining citizens in terms of, 23–24
  food dependence, 152–154, 159
  giving way to hierarchy in early modern Europe, 36–37
  importance to democratic success, 129–130
  Turkey's Gezi Park movement, 54–55
  See also self-sufficiency

Index

Index

Index

Index

Index

Index

Index

C. L. Skach is a professor of political science at the University of Bologna. She was previously professor of law at King's College London and professor of comparative government and law at the University of Oxford, and taught at Harvard University for nearly a decade. She splits her time between Bologna, Italy, and Oxford, UK.